AF352381

Equity in Education

Equity in Education

An International Comparison of Pupil Perspectives

Stephen Gorard
University of Birmingham, UK

Emma Smith
University of Birmingham, UK

With

David Greger and Dennis Meuret

First published 2010 by
PALGRAVE MACMILLAN

Palgrave Macmillan in the UK is an imprint of Macmillan Publishers Limited, registered in England, company number 785998, of Houndmills, Basingstoke, Hampshire RG21 6XS.

Palgrave Macmillan in the US is a division of St Martin's Press LLC, 175 Fifth Avenue, New York, NY 10010.

Palgrave Macmillan is the global academic imprint of the above companies and has companies and representatives throughout the world.

Palgrave® and Macmillan® are registered trademarks in the United States, the United Kingdom, Europe and other countries.

ISBN: 978–0–230–23025–5 hardback

This book is printed on paper suitable for recycling and made from fully managed and sustained forest sources. Logging, pulping and manufacturing processes are expected to conform to the environmental regulations of the country of origin.

A catalogue record for this book is available from the British Library.

A catalog record for this book is available from the Library of Congress.

10 9 8 7 6 5 4 3 2 1
19 18 17 16 15 14 13 12 11 10

Printed and bound in Great Britain by
CPI Antony Rowe, Chippenham and Eastbourne

Contents

Tables

Preface

The objective of this book is to document young people's experiences of justice in schools and beyond, and to relate these experiences to the development of their personal sense of justice and the criteria they use to decide whether something is fair or not. One particular concern was to represent the views and experiences of potentially disadvantaged pupils, including those with learning difficulties, or behavioural problems, those apparently less suited to an academic 'trajectory', recent immigrants, those learning through a second language, or who are from socioeconomically deprived backgrounds. We have now conducted a series of studies in six European countries, representing Northern, Southern, and Eastern Europe, and a comparative study in Japan. A comparative approach was used, because it allowed us to consider the natural variation in school organisation as a potential cause of any differences in the developing sense of justice among disadvantaged pupils. Our analysis considers the characteristics of the schools that pupils attend, the pupils' own family and social background, their indicators of disadvantage, and their developing sense of justice. We examine their experiences and the potential impact of their experiences on well-being, work, relations at school, involvement in tasks, and results, plus perseverance in school, ethical and civic judgements, trust in institutions, and unfairness in general. This provides important indications for policy-makers and practitioners about the role of school organisation, and the behaviour of teachers, in creating equity and helping to form pupils' sense of justice.

Pupils have quite clear views on what is fair, and are generally willing and able to express those views. Are research users willing to acknowledge and act on those views?

Much of the empirical work presented in this book has come from our research as part of the European Group on Research into Equity in Education Systems. In addition to all our colleagues whose names are listed below, we would like to acknowledge the principal contribution of Luciano Benadusi and Marc Demeuse. We also thank Karel Cerny for his coding of country of origin which is used in a section of Chapter 8, and Bernadette Giot for her contribution to the case study work outlined in Chapter 9.

The authors wish to convey their gratitude to the European Commission's representatives for their support throughout the project, especially Jean-Yves Stefani and Anders Hingel. We would also like to thank the Daiwa Anglo Japanese Foundation for supporting the Japanese part of the study and to our colleagues in the Kyoto University of Education, especially Dr Mizuyama Mitsuharu, for their help in undertaking the fieldwork.

A project supported by the European Commission
Directorate General of Education and Culture
Project Socrates 2005-2434/001-001 SO2-61OBGE

We would also like to thank all who took part in the study, especially our colleagues:

Nathanael Friant
Aletta Grisay
Christian Monseur
Frederique Artus
Giuseppe Ricotta
Norberto Bottani
Orazio Giancola
Sophie Desvignes
Vanita Sundaram

Part I

Introduction

1
Reconsidering What Schools Are For

Introduction

A key objective of education development is to increase participation and achievement among school pupils, especially those facing disadvantage in terms of language, poverty, ability, and special needs. Another is to enhance their enjoyment of learning and their preparation for citizenship. Much education research concerns achievement and participation. But less effort has been put into considering how to promote the experiences of fairness, enjoyment, and 'good' citizenship, and how to recognise success or failure in this. We add to knowledge in this area by looking at the impact of schools and pupil experience on how pupils might develop the civic 'values' of fairness, aspiration, and trust, by presenting the results of a new international survey of young people, using an instrument assessing their experiences of justice at school, home, and in wider society, their backgrounds, and their hopes for the future.

This book documents young people's experiences of justice in schools and beyond, relating these experiences to the development of their personal sense of justice and the criteria they use to decide whether something is fair or not. For many pupils, their experience of school is fundamental to their conception of wider society, their place as citizens, and their sense of justice (Gorard 2007a). We look at schools as organised societies and the part they play in creating a sense of justice among pupils. One particular concern was to represent the views and experiences of potentially disadvantaged pupils, including those with learning difficulties, or behavioural problems, those apparently less suited to an academic 'trajectory', plus recent immigrants, those learning through a second language, or who are from socioeconomically deprived backgrounds. We know from previous studies (our own and the wider literature) that these indicators of potential disadvantage are strongly linked to individual pupil attainment (Gorard and Smith 2004). But more generally it seems 'information about the position of the most disadvantaged groups in education is extremely scarce and fragmented. Genuine comparative research in this respect at the EU level is currently impossible because the basic information is not available' (Nicaise 2000, p. 314). More research was needed on the effectiveness of school reforms in tackling educational and social exclusion. We considered it essential for the benefit of policy-makers and practitioners that we ask pupils and listen to their own accounts of school and wider experiences.

We were interested in describing how schools create citizens – through formal teaching, as well as in their encouragement of pupil participation in community activities, democratic structures and inclusive arrangements. We were thus concerned with learning that is not entirely attainment-focused, but that may have ramifications for pupils' actions and trajectories in wider society. If we view schools as micro-societies we might surmise that the learning of justice and fairness in school will help shape young people's notions of justice outside school. Whatever the school system, we know that disadvantaged pupils tend to make less progress than other pupils during any given school phase, especially where they are clustered together (Duru-Bellat and Mingat 1997), perhaps because they have poorer learning conditions than other pupils (Grisay 1997). Thus, pupils' experiences of justice and, especially, injustice could undermine their interpersonal and institutional trust, promote passive attitudes towards political and civic participation, generate intolerance towards others who are clearly 'different', and even lead them to doubt whether an equitable existence is possible.

Starting from equality of access, that is, the right of everyone – whatever their origin – to attend school and moving then to equality of treatment, which consists of offering identical service to all, modern society has become increasingly demanding vis-à-vis its schools, and now expects greater equality of threshold outcomes as well. Thus, in most developed countries, the expectations from schooling are that all pupils will achieve equal performances at the end of a period of education, at least in the sense of mastery of basic (i.e., threshold) competencies considered indispensable for contemporary life. Naturally, this should not restrain some, or even many, from pursuing a school career beyond compulsory education.

Developing equity indicators for education

The discourse of economic competitiveness, via the Lisbon agenda in Europe, for example, has led to a considerable emphasis on international educational indicators, benchmarks and quality controls. In many areas 'by measuring the outcomes of national educational policies with indicators set at the EU level, rankings of the Member States are an intended outcome of the work programme' on indicators (Ertl 2006, p. 16). According to some, the building of comparable indicators is a powerful way of formulating educational policy without legislation, even though the European Maastricht treaty explicitly prohibited harmonisation of education and training policies. Whatever their downsides (Gorard 2001), international studies of different school systems can be valuable in highlighting the differences between countries and regions in the extent to which pupils are clustered by socioeconomic status or ability and the link between this and pupils' experiences of justice. International comparisons allow researchers to broaden their understanding of the impact of new policies, by comparing changes in countries in which a policy is active, with changes in a country unaffected by that policy. They present, in effect, a kind of natural and ethical experimental control.

Through data resulting from international surveys it has been possible to design indicators which describe the manner in which education systems treat the young generation for which they are responsible (Baye et al. 2006, OECD 2005). Whereas initial research work in this area tended to emphasise the effectiveness of education systems in generating test and attainment results, an interest in equity has gradually developed. At first this was based on the available documents – such as the OECD's Education at a Glance – but this led very quickly to creating specifically tailored evidence (Baye 2005, Gibson and Meuret 1995).

Following on from the work already undertaken by the Ad Hoc Group on Equity Issues of the OECD's Internal Education Indicators Project (INES) (Hutmacher et al. 2001), the European Group for Research on Equity in Educational Systems (EGREES 2005) proposed a reference framework allowing data to be organised into a coherent system of indicators (Demeuse 2004, Meuret 2001, Nicaise et al. 2005). A set of indicators was needed to grasp the complexity of education systems in regard to equity. The framework for a set of equity indicators was organised according to two dimensions. The first concerned the groups between which unjust differences may appear, such as where the gap between the weakest and the strongest performers is judged to be unacceptable, and for identifiable groups of pupils such as girls and boys, immigrants and indigenous, youngsters whose parents hold less distinguished/less well paid/less qualified professions and other more favoured pupils. The second dimension considered areas where such differences can appear, including

the external context, like poverty, and aspirations influenced by family and peers;

the education process itself, in terms of differences in the length or quality of education received, personal development, and differences in school compositions;

outcomes, such as the individual consequences of education like disparities in income, economic and social inequalities, social mobility, and collective benefits such as increased tolerance towards schools or others.

Of interest here were the OECD-funded Programme for International Pupil Assessment (PISA) studies, conducted in 2000 and 2003 (OECD 2007b). The first study covered 265,000 15-year-old pupils from 32 countries. The second covered 275,000 15-year-old pupils from 41 countries. The survey items included tests in literacy, maths, science, and problem-solving, as well as pupil and school questionnaires on aspects of pupil motivation, use of ICT, school organisation and so on. Following a re-analysis of the PISA 2000 results (EGREES 2005), we have previously conducted a follow-up survey with 6000 pupils in the same age range as PISA in five EU countries, focusing less on attainment (also the focus of the Third International Maths and Science Study), and more on pupils' own views of justice at and beyond school (Smith and Gorard 2006).

Large-scale international studies such as the IEA Civic Education Study have already sought to gain a clearer understanding of pupils' concepts of democracy and citizenship and how this varies across different nations. The 1999 phase of the Civic Education Study surveyed around 120,000 pupils aged 14 and 17–18 (Civic Education Study 2001). One key finding to emerge from this study was that schools that modelled democratic values by promoting an open climate for discussion were more likely to be effective in promoting both civic knowledge and civic engagement among their pupils (Torney-Purta et al. 2001). While there are many lessons to be learnt from studies of this type that can help us understand how pupils construct their notions of fairness and responsibility, their focus tends to be exclusively on issues of civic responsibility and civic engagement outside the school. Our interest here is to examine also how systems of fairness and equity operate to influence pupils' perspectives within their schools, and so their understanding of education in general.

For the new study described in this book, we conducted fieldwork in five European countries, representing Northern, Southern and Eastern Europe, and one Pacific Rim country (Japan). Our chief source of data is an international survey of the views of 14-year-old pupils. The instrument used was developed from that used in a large relevant pilot survey conducted by the researchers, benefiting from the lessons thereby learned, particularly in the clarification of the target disadvantaged groups. Around 14,000 pupils in around 450 schools took part. We collated existing official data about the intake and performance of these schools where available and supplemented these with a classroom-level questionnaire and with observations and field notes taken during administration of the survey. We use these various contextual sources as illustrations and potential explanations of the findings from the pupils. We describe differences in outcomes and experiences between socioeconomic and language groups, countries and school types. We have also modelled the plausible social and educational determinants of the different perceptions of justice among different types of pupils. The results have been presented to an international audience of teachers, school leaders and teacher trainers for discussion and feedback both on the presentation of results and on further analyses to be conducted. The comments and concerns of these practitioners have been integrated into our analysis as far as possible.

The structure of the book

What is equity in education, and why should we re-consider what schools are for? International studies of schooling usually focus on a rather narrow, though important, interpretation of pupil attainment. Policy-makers and other commentators want answers to questions such as how well their pupils are doing, how we can improve their scores, how well different sub-groups of pupils are doing in comparative terms, and what kind of school systems yield the best results. This traditional view of school effectiveness in re-considered in Chapter 2, suggesting that this whole field of work has become dominated by a flawed and unfruitful definition of what it means to be a good school or a good pupil.

In fact, schools and the people in them are about much more than 'pencil-and-paper' test scores. Chapters 3 and 4 consider schools as societies, both in themselves and as pupil preparation for wider society, and summarise some of the existing evidence on these matters. In particular, we present evidence that experiences at school have lifelong impacts on some pupils. The concept of equity, as the principle of justice underlying different criteria for justice such as equality of treatment and equality of outcome, is discussed in Chapter 5. The differing criteria for justice which are identified there would lead to contradictory claims and calls for action, unless it is clearly recognised that they are domain-specific. Do pupils recognise and apply these criteria in the same way? Chapters 5 and 6 describes our approach to researching these issues on an international stage, based in one East Asian and five European countries.

Chapters 7 to 10 summarise our important findings. The international comparative picture is presented in Chapter 7. Chapter 8 examines experience of justices for different, and potentially vulnerable, groups of pupils. Chapter 9 tells the story of pupils educated outside mainstream schools, and Chapter 10 puts this all together in a multivariate analysis, modelling the possible determinants of a selection of pupil-reported outcomes such as aspiration, trusting others, and notions of justice. Chapter 11 presents the implications of the study for policy, practice and the ways in which we might set about dealing with equity and education in the future.

2
Querying the Traditional Role of Schools in Attainment

Introduction

In this chapter we briefly rehearse the traditional way in which schools are judged – in terms of their 'effectiveness' at promoting the attainment of pupils in formal tests and assessments. In fact, so dominant is this view of the purpose and quality of schools that the impact of schools on pupil academic attainment is somewhat taken for granted, and the impact of schools on other potential outcomes is largely ignored. Later in the book we examine some of the other possible ways in which teachers, schools, and school structures can influence the development of pupils. Schools could be considered 'effective' in terms of financial efficiency, pupil attendance, pupil enjoyment of education, future pupil participation in education, pupil aspiration, preparation for citizenship and so on. Another perfectly proper indicator of school success can be based on pupil scores in assessments intended to discover how much or how well pupils have learnt what is taught in the school. What is interesting is how dominant this last version of school effectiveness has become over the last 50 years, in the United Kingdom and elsewhere. This chapter looks at the dominant approach to evaluating school performance, presenting flaws in its logic, and so arguing that it is time to stop using this now traditional but limited view of what schools are for. One consequence could be the opening of a revised approach to school design and allocation, based more on equity than on effectiveness as judged in these rather narrow terms. A fuller version of the discussion in this chapter appears in Gorard (2010a).

The school effectiveness model

There are a number of valid possible reasons for wanting to be able to judge school performance in terms of pupil attainment outcomes. In most countries, the majority of schools are publicly funded (see Chapter 5), and so the custodians of public finance will want to assess how well that money is being used. Policy-makers will be interested in how well this public service is working, and what the impact has been of any recent reforms. Parents and pupils might want to use a measure of school quality when making educational choices. Heads and teachers might want feedback on what is working well and what is in need of improvement at their own schools. Few of these stakeholders, using this perspective, tend to focus directly on the pupils and their experiences of school.

For any set of schools, if we rank them by their pupil scores in assessments of learning then we tend to find that schools at the high and low ends differ in more than their pupil assessments. Schools in areas with more expensive housing, and in the United States with more local income, schools that select their pupil intake by ability, aptitude or even religion, and schools requiring parents to pay for their child's attendance, are more prevalent among the high scores. Schools with high pupil mobility, often in inner-cities, taking high proportions of children living in poverty or with a different home language to the language of instruction, may be more prevalent among the low scores. This is well known, and means that raw-score indicators are not a fair test of school performance. Some early studies of school effectiveness famously found very little or no difference at all in the outcomes of schools once these kinds of pupil intake differences had been taken into account (Coleman et al. 1966). Such studies, using either or both of pupil prior attainment and pupil family background variables, have continued since then (Coleman et al. 1982, Gorard 2000a), and continue today (Guldemond and Bosker 2009, Lubienski and Lubienski 2006). The differences in pupil outcomes between individual schools, and types and sectors of schools, can be largely explained by the differences in their pupil intakes. The larger the sample, the better the study, and the more reliable the measures involved, then the higher percentage of raw-score difference between schools that can be explained by these pupil background variables (Shipman 1997, Tymms 2003). Looked at in this way, it seems that which school a pupil attends makes little difference to their learning (as assessed by these means, and compared to other schools in the same system). The variation in school outcomes unexplained by pupil background is deemed to be largely the messy stuff left over by the process of analysis.

However, over the past 30 years a different series of studies has come to a rather different conclusion, based on pretty much the same kind of evidence but with more emphasis on the prior attainment of pupils rather than their family background (Rutter et al. 1979). 'School effectiveness' researchers have accepted that much or most of the variation in school outcomes is due to school intake characteristics. But they have proposed that the residual variation (any difference in raw-scores left unexplained by pupil intake) is evidence of differential school and teacher effectiveness (e.g., Gray and Wilcox 1995, Kyriakides 2008, Nuttall et al. 1989). This second view has tended to prevail among education researchers outside the sociology of education tradition, and in government policy in developed countries (Sanders 2000). The variation in school outcomes unexplained by pupil background is deemed large enough, robust and invariant enough over time, to be accounted a school 'effect'. And teachers, schools and leaders are held accountable for the size of these effects. League tables, and report cards or similar, are published based on these school effects, and families are encouraged to use the results in selecting schools for their children.

In England, the Department for Children, Schools and Families (DCSF) is responsible for the organisation of schools' and childrens' services. DCSF (2007) rightly report that in comparing the performance of schools we must recognise that pupils have different starting points when arriving at any school, that schools have different proportions of pupils at any starting point, and that other external factors will affect the progress made by pupils. They conclude from this that their Contextual Value Added analysis (CVA) 'gives a much fairer statistical measure of the effectiveness of a school, and provides a *solid* basis for comparisons' (p. 2, emphasis added). Using CVA results, school inspection grades are partly pre-determined, schools are lauded or criticised, and league tables are created to assist parental choice (see later section). How does this CVA work? An extended case study discussion of CVA follows to establish that it, like all traditional approaches to school effectiveness, cannot work. This means that an entirely new way of thinking about the effectiveness of schools is possible and indeed necessary. It is this new way of thinking that forms the basis for the rest of this book. Readers already familiar with the inherent problems of school effectiveness may wish to skip to the final section of this chapter.

CVA is based on a value-added (VA) score for each pupil's attainment, calculated as the difference between their own outcome point score and the median outcome score for all pupils with the same prior (input) score. For example, in Key Stage 2 to Key Stage 4 CVA, the average points score at KS2 is calculated for all KS4 pupils in all maintained schools (and non-maintained special schools) in England. Key Stage 2 leads to statutory testing at the end of primary education, usually for pupils aged 10. Key Stage 4 leads to assessment at age 16, currently the legal age at which a pupil can leave school. The average is of the Key Stage 2 scores ('fine grades') for each pupil in three core subjects (English, maths, and science). Then the 'best 8' (capped GCSE equivalent) KS4 score is calculated for each pupil. These figures yield the median KS4 score for each KS2 score. The difference between the median and the actual KS4 score for each pupil is their individual VA score. This difference is adjusted for the individual pupil characteristics, including sex, special needs, ethnicity, eligibility for free school meals (FSM), first language, mobility, precise age, whether in care, and an area-based measure of the proportion of households on low income (IDACI – an index of deprivation), among other things. The full formula appears as the Appendix to this book. Equivalent models apply to CVA calculations for other stages of schooling, such as KS1 to KS2.

Errors in the data

This kind of calculation of pupil progress appears very clear, if somewhat complex, and the logic seems plausible. School effectiveness models like CVA take the prior attainment and context of the pupil into account in order to judge pupil progress during one phase of schooling. This should be a better measure of relative success than the raw-score results. Of course, the process depends heavily on the quality of the data used in the calculation. If the data is complete, correct, and an excellent measure of what it is intended to measure, then the process of calculating school effects in this way looks and sounds as though it has merit. Unfortunately, the kinds of datasets used for the job are necessarily incomplete, and contain both inaccuracies and errors in measurement. This section continues the example of CVA as an illustration of the range and importance of these errors in a real-life situation. The following section then shows how these errors propagate through the process of computation, making the results of school effectiveness calculations meaningless.

The first consideration is the completeness of the kinds of data needed for school effectiveness calculations. CVA in England is calculated using two linked official datasets – the National Pupil Database (NPD) and the Pupil Level Annual School Census (PLASC). All schools are required by law to provide figures for these in each school year, further data is added from existing official sources, and funding for the school hinges on their completion. PLASC contains a record for every pupil in maintained schools in England, detailing their background characteristics, including periods in-care, special needs status and first language. It also has some attainment data. NPD holds individual records on every pupil in maintained schools in England, detailing their examination and assessment entry and attainment, and also has some background data. They provide a wonderful and welcome resource for the researcher, at least the equal of equivalent datasets in other developed countries. Nevertheless, the records are not complete.

There are missing cases in the data, some by design such as those 7% of pupils attending private schools, and those educated at home. In addition, there will be a small number of cases in transition between schools, or otherwise not in, or registered for, a school. The latter includes quite a high proportion of those pupils permanently excluded from school. For example in 2005 over 3000 pupils who had been permanently excluded from school were missing from PLASC (Smith 2009). Further, although both databases ostensibly contain records for all other pupils, in some years around 10% of the individual pupil records are un-matched across the two databases. This means, of course, that their background and attainment data cannot be matched. The same thing happens trying to match cases across phases of schooling for the same pupils. In 2007 for example, the dataset for the Key Stage 4 (KS4 or 15-year-old) cohort contained records for 673,563 pupils, but nearly 10% of these could not be matched with the records of the same pupils from an earlier Key Stage such as KS2 (when they were 10-year-olds in their final year of primary school). Any pupil moving to or from one of the other home countries of the United Kingdom such as Wales, where some statutory testing has been abolished, will have missing scores for one or more Key Stages. Any pupil moving from a private school, from a non-formal educational setting, or from outside the United Kingdom will similarly have no matching record of prior attainment at school on the PLASC/NPD system. In summary, perhaps nearly 10% of children will be missing from the databases completely, up to 10% will have a missing prior attainment record, and up to 10% will not have a matched record in either PLASC or NPD. There will be some overlap between these missing cases, but this already represents a far from complete dataset.

A second consideration is the data missing even from those cases that do have records in the databases. In the 2007 PLASC/NPD datasets used to calculate CVA, every KS4 variable, including both the contextual and attainment variables, had a high proportion of missing cases. For example, whether a pupil was in-care had at least 80,278 values missing (12% of all cases). At least 75,944 were missing a code for free school meal eligibility (an important indicator of family poverty for CVA purposes). This represents over 11% of cases. Even when data does not appear as missing, it can be effectively missing. For example, the data on pupil ethnic background has data appearing as 'system missing' but in addition some pupils have ethnicity not coded as missing but as 'Refused' or 'Not obtained'. There is again some overlap between these missing cases, but only some. For example, if we delete from the 2007 PLASC/NPD all cases missing data on FSM, in-care, special needs, sex and/or ethnicity data then the database drops in size to 577,115 pupils (or 85% of its apparent size, which was already itself incomplete as explained above). If we consider *all* of the variables used in CVA (see Appendix), including further contextual variables such as pupil first language, and the attainment scores for each subject and grade (there are many of these), less than 50% of the children of England in any age cohort have a record in all relevant databases that is complete in terms of all key variables.

One of the reasons for using area-based measures such as the index of deprivation (IDACI) in CVA is that they can replace missing data for individuals to some extent. However, this geographical approach suffers from two clear defects. First, it introduces a kind of ecological fallacy by assuming that everyone has the modal characteristics of the other people in the area where they live (Webber and Butler 2007). Second, it relies on knowing the post code (area or ZIP code) of all individuals anyway. In the 2007 PLASCC/NPD, at least 69,902 (well over 10%) of the IDACI scores are missing because the address of the pupil is unknown. This then also introduces a clear error in at least one variable for *all* pupil records. The IDACI scores for all pupils, and as used in the CVA model, are calculated on the basis of scores for all households in England. Then we need to realise that all of this missing data occurs not only in the KS4 datasets when the pupil is 15 or 16 but also in any other matched dataset such as KS2 used for the prior attainment scores when the pupil was aged 10 or 11. It is clear that missing data is a huge problem for any analysis of PLASC/NPD.

In practice, missing cases are simply ignored, and missing values are replaced with a default substitute – usually the mean score or modal category (and male for sex of pupil). So, the DCSF analysts assume that pupils without IDACI scores (usually because they have no post code) live in average income neighbourhoods, and that where we do not know when a pupil joined their present school we should assume that they have been in attendance for a long time. Anyone whose eligibility for FSM is not known is assumed not to be living in poverty, anyone without a KS2 or KS4 examination score is an average attainer, and so on. These kinds of assumptions have to be made in order not to lose the high number of cases with at least one missing value in a critical variable. But these are very questionable assumptions. There is plenty of evidence of differences between pupils with complete and incomplete values in such datasets (Amrein-Beardsley 2008). And making these unjustified assumptions then means that a very high proportion of cases is likely to have an incorrect value in at least one critical variable. In general, missing data is a serious problem to calculation of value-added using any model and for any country (Van de Grift 2009).

How good then is the data that is not missing? Assessment via examination, project, coursework or teacher's grading is an imperfect process. There are huge and well-documented issues of comparability in assessment scores between years of assessment, curriculum subjects, modes of assessment, examining boards, and types of qualifications (among other issues, see Gorard 2000b, Newton 1997, Nuttall 1979). Newton (2009, p. 181) says:

> There is no doubt that a substantial percentage of pupils would receive different levels were the testing process to be replicated within any particular year for any particular test

Outcries over mistakes in statutory assessment are frequent in England. A recent press report says:

> Nearly half of pupils taking national tests in English writing are awarded the wrong grade because of inaccurate marking, newly published research says. (Stewart 2009, p. 14)

The year before this, the regulatory body for examinations in England – the Qualifications and Curriculum Authority (QCA) – had been broken up after another very public failure, and its chief resigned. Yet the checks made by its successor – OFQUAL – to avoid similar mistakes have been cut further, presumably because of funding difficulties. In fact, public assessment is generally handled well in England, and the kinds of high-profile errors made by QCA and others are understandable in the light of a complex national testing and regulatory system (see below). To some extent these problems are coming to light because key figures at QCA decided that the public should be a given a more realistic picture of what test and examination 'standards' mean. Moderation will be imperfect and mistakes will be made. But if in any one year up to half of the grades given in one test could be admitted to be in error, then we must assume a reasonable level of error in any assessment data of the kind used to calculate CVA.

Even when the system correctly assigns grades to pupils in their assessments we cannot be sure that they are free from error for a number of reasons. If we take the underlying competence of the pupil as the true measure wanted in an assessment, even a perfect assessment instrument could lead to error in the achieved measure due to differences in the setting for the assessment (a fire alarm going off in one examination hall, for example), time of day, inadvertent (and sometimes deliberate) teacher assistance, the health of the candidate, and so on. Competence is not an easy thing to measure, unlike the length of the examination hall or the number of people in it. However well-constructed the assessment system is, we must assume a reasonable level of measurement error in the results.

Then the analyst is faced with issues of aggregation and comparability. For example, the KS4 analysis involves GCSEs handled by different examining boards, sometimes taken via modules in different years, and for all different subjects and tiers of entry. Some GCSEs will be short and some full. Even if an analyst is fairly sure about the comparability and reliability of such scores, these will have to be aggregated with results from an increasing number of different qualifications. In 2007, these included GNVQ Intermediate, NVQ, National Certificate in Business, BTEC, Key Skills, Basic Skills, and Asset Language Units. These all have to be converted to the common 'currency' of point scores, despite the fact that their grading structures are completely different. This aggregation to 'best 8' points scores adds further inaccuracies to those catalogued so far.

The same kind of consideration applies to any contextual variables. Even in NPD/PLASC with a simple binary code for sex, a few pupils are coded as male in one and female in the other database (more have nothing coded, and one or two have an invalid code, presumably from a data entry error). The error component in variables such as FSM, ethnicity, first language, and perhaps most particularly special educational needs (SEN), is even greater. Special educational needs, for example, are represented by a variable having three possible sources (School Action, Action Plus, or a statement). Some of these are the responsibility of the school, and some are sensitive to the actions of parents motivated to gain extra time in examinations for their children. The number of pupils with recorded SEN shows huge variation over years in the same schools, and appear in very different proportions in different parts of

England (Gorard et al. 2003). Ethnic groups (based on 19 categories for CVA) are notoriously difficult to classify (Gorard 2008a). Here they are used in interaction with FSM eligibility (itself an incomplete measure). Where variables are used in interaction like this, to calculate CVA, an error in either one of them leads to an error in the combined result.

Once all of the relevant measurements have been achieved, they must be coded, entered and stored in the databases. Each of these steps introduces the likelihood of further errors (as illustrated in Gorard 2010a). At the end of all this it is hard to believe that any pupil record will be free from all errors, with so many areas for errors to creep into the data. CVA in England has been used as an illustration of the problems in the data even for an excellent dataset. Similar problems or worse appear in other official datasets in the United Kingdom (Gorard 2008b) and in other countries like the United States (Sanders and Horn 1998, p. 248). What happens to these errors in a school effectiveness calculation?

The propagation of errors

For any real measurement that we use for analysis we must assume the possibility of measurement error. Measurement error in this context means a difference between the ideal representation of something and our achieved measure. If someone actually has three children but our measurement claims that they have two children, then our measurement of the number of children is in error by one. This simple discrepancy is often termed the absolute error. A more useful way of envisaging such an error is as a fraction of the measurement itself – the relative error. In this example, the relative error is 1/2. In trying to measure 3 we achieve a measure of 2 which is out by 1. If we were out by 1 in attempting to measure the number of children in the entire country, this would not be such a serious measurement error, and the relative error would be much smaller than 1/2.

Imagine for the sake of argument that all measures such as pupil prior attainment used in CVA were only 90% accurate, having a relative error of 1/10. This would be very generous assumption given the real-life scale of errors discussed in the previous section. What would this mean? In itself, it tells us what we already know – that the score for any pupil cannot be guaranteed to be accurate. We should not treat a score of 70 for one pupil as being substantially different in practice from a score of 73 for another pupil. The difference between them is smaller than the error bound of each. On the other hand, it means that a score of 70 *can* be treated as substantially different from a score of 100, since the difference is greater than the error bound. Put another way an achieved score of 70 in the database could be between 63 and 77 in reality (+/− 10%). An achieved score of 100 could be between 90 and 110 in reality. Since 90 is still larger than 77 we can proceed with some confidence that the score represented by 100 really is larger than the score of 70. For normal descriptive purposes in education and social science a relative error of 10% in our achieved figures is acceptable. But what happens when we feed scores such as these into a school effectiveness calculation like CVA?

In England, the model for CVA used by the DCSF involves finding for all pupils 'the difference (positive or negative) between their predicted and actual attainment' (DCSF 2007, p. 7). The predicted attainment for any one pupil is based on the average gain score for all pupils with the same prior attainment (adjusted for contextual information). The difference between any pupil's predicted and actual attainment will tend to be insubstantial, because if the predicted and actual attainment scores were not very close for a majority of pupils then the model would not be any good. This means that the figure computed for the pupil value-added score is usually very small, perhaps even negligible, in comparison to the attainment scores from which it is calculated. CVA subtracts the predicted and actual attainment to create a much smaller figure, but adds their maximum errors (since we do not know if these errors are positive or negative).

For an illustration of the importance of this propagation of errors, imagine a pupil with an actual points score of 100 for attainment at KS4, but with a predicted points score of 99. The prediction is a good one in that it is close, but the pupil appears to have made marginally more progress than expected. Both scores are assumed to be 90% accurate (see above). This relative error of only 10% is a very conservative estimate given the multiple sources of error described in the previous section, and the scale of missing data. The predicted score, based on all of the CVA variables in isolation and in interaction will have a much larger error component than this in reality. But even an error of 10% means that the actual score for this pupil could be anywhere between 90 and 110 in reality, and the predicted score ought to be anywhere from 89.1 to 108.9. This means that the real residual score for this pupil (their CVA score) could be anything from +20.9 (110–89.1) to −18.9 (90–108.9). The maximum relative error in the calculated answer of +1 is 3.98 divided by 1. This is a massive 3,980%. By subtracting two similar numbers with an acceptable level of initial error (10%) we are left with an 'answer' composed almost entirely of error. We genuinely have no idea whether this pupil has done better or worse than expected. There is no way that such a result could be used for any practical purpose. If the initial relative error in either the actual or the predicted score is greater than 10%, as it almost certainly would be in reality, the error in the CVA result would be even greater.

Where the actual and predicted scores are the same for any pupil (i.e., when the CVA model works well), the residual score is zero and so the relative error in the result is infinite. As the achieved and predicted scores diverge the relative error in the residual tends to decline. But this then means that the CVA model, which is meant to make *accurate* predictions, is not working well. If the predictions are so far out that we can begin to ignore the error components is this better or worse for the school effectiveness model? In order to retain something like the relative error of 10% in the original scores, the CVA prediction would have to be out by a long way from the achieved result. For example, a predicted score of 50 for a pupil, with a 10% initial error, represents a range of 45 to 55. An actual score of 100 for the same pupil, with a 10% initial error, represents a range of 90 to 110. This means that the real residual score for this pupil (their CVA score) could be anything from +65 (110–45) to +35 (90–55). This yields a maximum relative error of 60% in the resulting CVA score of +50. So even when the CVA prediction is way out, as in this example, an initial error of 10% propagates to 60% via simple subtraction. If we assume that the school effectiveness model is capturing anything sensible at all, this pupil can be deemed to have done very well (or to have done very badly in the prior assessment, or both). This is true even if the maximum error applies. How can we tell whether any CVA score (for pupil, teacher, department, school, or area) is of this kind, where we cannot be sure about the precise figure but we can be sure that the result is so far away from that predicted as to dwarf any error component?

The failure of technical solutions to error

It is worth pointing out at this stage in the argument that any analysis using real data with some combination of the inevitable measurement errors described so far will lead to an incorrect result. Of course, the more accurate the measures are the closer to the ideal correct answer we can be. However, we have no reason to believe that any or all of these sources of error lead to random measurement error (of the kind that might come from random sampling variation, for example). Those refusing to take part in a survey, those not registered at school, those unwilling to reveal their family income or benefit (for free school meal eligibility purposes) cannot be imagined as some kind of random subset of the school population. Like every stage in the error generation process described so far, they are not random in nature, occurrence or source (Gorard 2010a).

Unfortunately the field of school effectiveness research works on the invalid assumption that errors in the data are random in nature and so can be estimated, and weighted for, by techniques based on random sampling theory. These techniques are fatally flawed, in their own terms, even when used 'correctly' with random samples (Gorard 2010b). The conditional probabilities generated by sampling theory tell us, under strict conditions and assumptions, how often random samples would generate a result as extreme or more extreme as the one we might be considering. The p-value in a significance test tells analysts the probability of observing a score as or more extreme, assuming that the score is actually no different from zero (and so that the divergence from zero is the result of random sampling variation alone). Of course, this conditional probability of the data given the nil-null hypothesis is not what the analysts want. In a school effectiveness context such as the ones outlined above, the analyst wants to know whether the CVA score (the residual, whether for individual or school) is large enough to take note of (to dwarf its relative error). They actually want the probability of the null hypothesis given the data they observed. They could convert the probability of the data to the probability of the hypothesis using Bayes' Theorem, as long as they already knew the underlying and unconditional probability of the null hypothesis anyway. But they cannot know the latter. So they pretend that the probability of the data given the null hypothesis is the same as, or closely related to, the probability of the null hypothesis given the data. They then use the p-value from significance tests to 'reject' the null hypothesis on which the p-value is predicated. This *modus tollens* kind of argument does not work with likelihoods, for a number of reasons, including Jeffrey's so-called paradox that a low probability for the data can be associated with a high probability for the null hypothesis, or a low one, or a mid-range value, and *vice versa*. It depends on the underlying probability of the null hypothesis – which we do not know.

So, even used as intended, p-values can not help most analysts in the school effectiveness (SE) field. The same applies to standard errors, and confidence intervals and their variants. But the situation is worse than this because in the field of school effectiveness, these statistical techniques based on sampling theory are hardly ever used *as intended*. Most commonly, the sampling techniques are used with population figures such as those from NPD/PLASC. In this context, the techniques mean nothing. There is no sampling variation to estimate when working with population data (whether for a nation, region, education authority, school, year, class, or social group). There are missing cases and values, and there is measurement error. But these are not generated by random sampling, and so sampling theory cannot estimate them, adjust for them, or help us decide how substantial they are in relation to our manifest data.

Despite all this, DCSF use and attempt to defend the use of confidence intervals with their population CVA data. A confidence interval, remember, is an estimate of the range of values that would be generated by repeated random sampling. It has no relevance at all to population data like PLASC/NPD. It is of no real use to an analyst, even when calculated for a random sample, for the same reasons as for p-values. And as with p-values, it does not even make sense to calculate a confidence interval for population data of any kind. Confidence intervals are therefore of no use in standard school effectiveness research, even though some purported authorities erroneously continue to propose the use of confidence intervals with school effectiveness scores based on population figures (e.g., Goldstein 2008).

In general, the field as a whole simply ignores these quite elementary logical problems, while devising more and more complex models comprehended by fewer and fewer people. Perhaps the most common inappropriate complex technique used in this field is multi-level (hierarchical linear) modelling. This technique was devised as one of many equivalent ways of overcoming the correlation between cases in cluster-randomised samples (Gorard 2009a). This, like all other techniques based on sampling theory, is of no consequence for school effectiveness work based on population figures. There are no samples. Advocates now claim that these complex models have other purposes – such as allowing analysts to partition variation in scores between levels such as individuals, schools and districts. But such partitioning can, like overcoming the inter-correlation in clusters, be done in other and generally simpler ways. Anyway, the technique is still pointless. Most such models do not use districts or areas as a level, and those that do tend to find little or no variation there once other levels have been accounted for (Smith and Street 2006, Tymms et al. 2008). The complexity gains us nothing, and loses the understanding of many of those most concerned with delivering effective education.

The minimal evidence of school impact on attainment

Why, if the foregoing is true, do so many analysts, policy-makers, users and practitioners seem to believe that school effectiveness yields useful and practical information? It is tempting to say that perhaps many of them have not really thought about the process and are simply impressed by what appears to be a scientific and technical solution to judging school performance. Part of the answer might also lie in the money to be made. In England, school effectiveness has become an industry, employing civil servants at DCSF and elsewhere, producing incentives for teachers deemed CVA experts in schools, creating companies and consultants to provide data analysis, paying royalties to software authors, and funding for academics from the taxpayer. A cynical view would be that most people in England do not understand CVA, and a high proportion of those that do stand to gain from its use in some way.

It is also possible that the problem stems from our lack of ability to calibrate the results of school effectiveness models against anything except themselves. In everyday measurements of time, length, temperature, and so on we get a sense of the accuracy of our measuring scales by comparing measurements with the qualities being measured (Gorard 2009b). There is no equivalent for CVA. The scores are just like magic figures emerging from a long-winded and quasi-rational calculation. Their advocates claim that these figures represent 'solid' and fair school performance measures, but they can provide nothing except the purported plausibility of the calculation to justify that. Supposing, for the sake of argument, that the calculation did not work for the reasons given so far in this chapter. What would we expect to emerge from it? The fact that the data is riddled with initial errors and that these propagate through the calculation does not mean that we should expect the results for all schools to be the same, once contextualised prior attainment is accounted for. The bigger the deviations between predicted and attained results, of the kind that SE researchers claim as evidence of effectiveness, the more this could also be evidence of the error component. In this situation, the bigger the error in the results the bigger the 'effect' might appear to be to some. So, we cannot improve our approach to get a bigger effect to outscore the error component. Whatever the residuals are we simply do not know if they are error or effect. We do know, however, that increasing the quality and scale of the data is associated with a decrease in the apparent school effect (Tymms 2003).

If the VA residuals were actually only error, how would the results behave? We would expect CVA results to be volatile and inconsistent over years and between key stages in the same schools. This is what we generally find (Hoyle and Robinson 2003, Kelly and Monczunski 2007, Tymms and Dean 2004). Of course, in any group of schools under consideration, some schools will have apparently consistent positive or negative CVA over a period of time. This, in itself, means nothing. Again imagine what we would expect if the 'effect' were actually all propagated error. Since CVA is zero-sum by design, around half of all schools in any one year must have positive scores and half negative. If the CVA were truly meaningless, then we might expect around one-quarter of all schools to have successive positive CVA scores over two years (and one-quarter negative). Again, this is what we find. *Post hoc*, we cannot use a run of similar scores to suggest consistency without consideration of what we would expect if the scores meant nothing. Thomas, Peng, and Gray (2007) looked at successive years of positive VA in one England district from 1993 to 2002. They seemed perplexed that 'it appears that only one in 16 schools managed to improve continuously for more than four years at some point over the decade in terms of value-added' (p. 261). Yet 1 in 16 schools with four successive positive scores is exactly how many would be predicted assuming that the scores mean nothing at all (since 2^{-4} equals 1/16).

A number of studies have found correlations of only around 0.5 and 0.6 over two to five years between VA scores for the same schools (Leckie and Goldstein 2009). This is a very low figure for practical use. A correlation of 0.5 after two years means that only 25% of the variation in VA is common to those years. Is this really any more than we would expect by chance? Whatever it is that is producing VA measures for schools, it is ephemeral. What is particularly interesting about this variability is that it does not appear in the raw-scores. Raw-scores for any school tend to be very similar from year to year, but the 'underlying' VA is not. Is this evidence that VA really changes that much and so quickly, or does it just illustrate again the central point that VA is very sensitive to the propagation of relative error, in a way that raw-scores are not?

The coefficients in the CVA model, fitted *post hoc* via multi-level regression, mean nothing in themselves. Even a table of complete random numbers can generate regression results as coherent (and convincing to some) as SE models (Gorard 2008a). With enough variables, combinations of variables and categories within variables it is possible to create a perfect multiple correlation ($R^2 = 1.00$) from completely nonsensical data. In this context, it is intriguing to note the observation by Glass (2004) that one school directly on a county line was attributed to both counties in the Tennessee Value Added Assessment System and two VA measures were calculated. The two results were completely different – suggesting perhaps that neither really meant anything at all. Even advocates and pioneers of school effectiveness admit that the data and models we have do not allow us to differentiate, in reality, between school performances. 'Importantly, when we account for prediction uncertainty, the comparison of schools becomes so imprecise that, at best, only a handful of schools can be significantly separated from the national average, or separated from any other school' (Leckie and Goldstein 2009, p. 16).

The key calculation underlying CVA is the creation of the residual between actual and predicted pupil scores. Since this is based on two raw-scores (the prior and current attainment of each pupil), it should not be surprising to discover that VA results are highly correlated with each of these raw-scores (Gorard 2006a, 2008c). The scale of this correlation is now routinely disguised by the contextual figures used in CVA, but it is still there. In fact, the correlation between prior and current attainment is the same size as the correlation between prior attainment and VA scores. Put more simply, VA calculations are flawed from the outset by not being independent enough of the raw-scores from which they are generated. They are no more a fair test of school performance than raw-scores are.

The damage caused by school effectiveness

Does any of this matter? Yes. Schools, heads and teachers are being routinely rewarded or punished on the basis of this kind of invalid evidence. Teachers are spending their time looking at things like departmental value-added figures and distorting their attention to focus on particular areas or types of pupils. School effectiveness results have been used to determine funding allocations and to threaten schools with closure (Bald 2006, Mansell 2006). The national school inspection system in England, run by OFSTED, starts with a CVA, and the results of that analysis partly pre-determine the results of the inspection (Gorard 2008c). Schools are paying public funds to external bodies for value-added analyses and breakdowns of their effectiveness data. Parents and pupils are being encouraged to use school effectiveness evidence (in league tables, for example) to judge their schools and potential schools. If the results are largely spurious this means a lot of time and money is wasted and, more importantly, pupils' education is being needlessly damaged.

However, the dangers of school effectiveness are even greater than this. School effectiveness is associated with a narrow understanding of what education is for. It encourages, unwittingly, an emphasis on assessment and test scores – and teaching to the test – because over time we tend to get the system we measure for and so privilege. And policies designed to improve test performance can lead to poorer school performance in other ways, such as pupil dropout or exclusion (Rumberger and Palardy 2005). Further, rather than opening information about schools to a wider public, the complexity of CVA and similar models excludes and so disempowers most people. These are the people who pay tax for, work in, or send their children to schools. Even academics are largely excluded from understanding and so criticising school effectiveness work (Normand 2008). Relevant academic work is often peer-reviewed and 'quality' checked by a relatively small clique. School effectiveness then tends to monopolise political expertise on schools and public discussion of education, even though most policy-makers, official bodies like OFSTED, and the public simply have to take the results on trust.

The widespread use of CVA for league tables, official DCSF performance data, and in models of school effectiveness also has the inadvertent impact of making it harder to examine how well schools are doing with different groups of pupils. One of the main reasons for initially setting up a free (taxpayer-funded), universal and compulsory system of schools was to try and minimise the influence of pupil family background. The achievement gaps between rich and poor, or between ethnic and language groups, give schools and society some idea of how well that equitable objective is being met. What CVA does is to recognise that these gaps exist but then makes them invisible by factoring them into the VA prediction. It no longer makes sense to ask whether the CVA is any different in a school or a school system for rich and poor, or different ethnic and language groups. DCSF (2007) appear to recognise this danger when they say (in bold, p. 2) 'CVA should not be used to set lower expectations for any pupil or group of pupils'. This means – bizarrely – that a school with a high level of poverty will be correctly predicted to have equivalently lower outcomes, but at the same time must not 'expect' lower outcomes.

It is also important to recall that VA, CVA and the rest are all zero-sum calculations. The CVA for a pupil, teacher, department, school, or district is calculated relative to all others. Thus, around half of all non-zero scores will be positive and half negative. Whether intentionally or not, this creates a system clearly based on competition. A school could improve its results and still have negative CVA if everyone else improved as well. A school could even improve its results and get a worse CVA than before. The whole system could improve and half of the schools would still get negative CVA. Or all schools could get worse and half would still get positive CVA scores. And so on. It is not enough to do well. Others have to fail for any school to obtain a positive result. Or more accurately, it is not even necessary to do well at all; it is only necessary to not do as badly as others. This is a ridiculous way of calculating school performance *sui generis*, as shown in this chapter so far. But why, in particular, design this kind of monitoring system and at the same time ask schools in England to form partnerships and federations, and to co-operate more in the delivery of KS3 and the 14–19 Reform Programme?

Even worse, in some countries like the United States, the same kind of data and associated analyses are being used to decide on the purported effectiveness of individual teachers. For example, since at least 1996, Sanders and others (Sanders 2000, Sanders and Horn 1998, Sanders and Rivers 1996) have claimed to be able to estimate teacher effectiveness from pupil test scores. The claimed result is that 'Our research work... clearly indicates that differences in teacher effectiveness is [*sic*] the single largest factor affecting academic growth of populations of pupils' (Sanders 2000, p. 334). Their Tennessee Value-added Assessment System (TVAAS) has been described as 'an efficient and effective method for determining individual teacher's influence on the rate of academic growth for pupil populations' (Sanders and Rivers, p. 1). It uses the academic test scores of pupils, tracked longitudinally, in a complex statistical analysis, to estimate the impact of their teachers. Barber and Mourshed (2007) call the research by Sanders 'seminal' in showing how important effective teachers are, and how damaging poor teachers are, for pupil learning. They conclude that the quality of instruction in education is paramount, and therefore that the preparation of teachers is a key determinant of education quality. This research 'finding' is now reflected in some important policy documents, including those of the European Commission.

TVAAS uses the 'scaled scores' of pupils (Sanders and Horn 1998, p. 249) over time (usually an average of three years) in each curriculum area to calculate gain scores, also referred to as a pupil's progress. The TVAAS work attributes variation in these residuals to teacher effects alone, even though, as illustrated in the chapter so far, the vast majority of variation could more honestly be attributed to propagation of initial errors. As shown, these errors are large when dealing with 'school' effectiveness, analysing results for an entire cohort and treating all subject areas as equivalent for analytic purposes, yielding 100 cases or more per school. Teacher effectiveness on the other hand, attempts to measure progress in terms of individual school subjects and teachers. The largest number of cases involved is likely to be a teaching group of around 30 pupils or less. Irrespective of all other factors, this will make teacher effectiveness scores even more volatile than purported school effects, because of the small numbers involved.

What is left from the residual apart from error could be attributed to teachers, but also external determinants such as the continuing influence of differential family support, socioeconomic trajectories, and cultural and ethnic-related factors, plus school-level factors such as resources, curricula, timetabling and leadership, educational factors beyond the school, such as district and area policies and funding arrangements. Of course, all such attributions have no more justification that an attribution of the residual gain scores to the impact of teachers. But they are all in competition to explain the same small amount of variation (once prior attainment is accounted for).

Anyway not all areas of teaching are routinely subject to statutory testing in Tennessee or elsewhere (Sanders and Horn 1998). Even in England which has a famously prescriptive programme of statutory testing at ages 7, 11, and 14, the focus is largely on maths, science and English. This means that some teachers cannot be included anyway since their subject contributions are not tested for (most obviously perhaps sports staff). It is very rare for one pupil to come into contact with only one teacher, even for one subject. Team-teaching, teaching assistants, on-line and virtual participation, and replacement and pupil teachers, among other factors, will confuse the issue. Teachers and their styles might vary over time, and might be effective for some pupils but not others. Their effectiveness might depend on the precise topic taught.

Sanders and Horn (1998, p. 254) claim that 'African American pupils and white pupils with the same level of prior achievement make comparable academic progress when they are assigned to teachers of comparable effectiveness'. What does this mean? The teacher effectiveness is calculated on the basis of the progress made by pupils, so this claim by Sanders and Horn is tautological. In fact their whole argument about the importance and impact of teachers is circular. Effective teachers are defined as those with pupils making good progress, so obviously, but by definition only, pupils make good progress with effective teachers. Empirically, this means nothing, even when dressed up in the most complex of (invalid and exclusionary) statistical analyses. The tautology at the heart of teacher effectiveness work like this makes it scientifically dishonest.

The whole-school effectiveness model, as currently imagined, should be abandoned. It clearly does not and could not work as intended, so it causes all of the damage and danger described above for no good reason. It continues partly as a kind of voodoo science (Park 2000), wherein adherents prefer to claim they are dealing with random events, making it easier to explain away the uncertainty and unpredictability of their results. But it also continues for the same reasons as it was created in the first place. We want to be able to measure school performance, and we know that mere raw-score figures tell us largely about the school intake. However, we must not continue with school effectiveness once aware of its flaws simply because we cannot imagine what to do instead. For some examples of possible alternatives, see Gorard (2010a).

Pupil prior attainment and background explain the vast majority of variation in school outcomes. This finding is clear because its scale and consistency over time and place dwarfs the error component in the calculation (largely because the error does not have a chance to propagate in the same way as for CVA analysis). Why is this not more clearly understood and disseminated by politicians? Policy-makers in England have built a system of maintained schools that remains loosely comprehensive, and is funded quite equitably (more so than the United States, for example), on a per-pupil basis adjusted for special circumstances. The curriculum is largely similar (the National Curriculum) for ages 5 to 14 at least, taught by nationally recognised teachers with Qualified Teacher Status, inspected by a national system (OFSTED), and assessed by standardised tests up to Key Stage 3. Education is compulsory for all, and free at the point of delivery. In a very real sense it sounds as though it would not matter much which school a pupil attends, in terms of qualifications as an outcome. And indeed, that is what decades of research have shown is true.

Are pupils and their parents being misled into thinking that which school they use does make a substantial difference? Perhaps, or perhaps qualifications at age 16 are not what parents and pupils are looking for when they think of a new school for a child aged 4 or even 10. Or perhaps parents are smarter than policy-makers, realising that current VA scores for any school or phase are historical and tell them only what might have happened if their child had started at that school five years ago. School choice research suggests that what families are really looking for is safety and happiness for their children (Gorard 1997). When thinking about moving a 10-year-old from a small primary school in which they are the oldest to a much larger, more distant secondary school with pupils up to the age of 19, security is often the major concern. This is why proximity can be seen as a rational choice. It is also possible that parents know perfectly well that raw-scores are not an indication of the quality of the school attended but of the other pupils attending. Using raw-scores might be a rational way for a lay person to identify a school in which learning was an important part of everyday school life. Raw-scores, like behaviour at the school bus stop, are used as a proxy indication of school intake.

If so, several conclusions might follow. Politicians could disseminate the truth that in terms of traditional school outcomes it makes little difference which school a pupil attends. This might reduce the allure of specialisms, selection by aptitude or attainment, faith-based schools, and other needlessly divisive elements for a national school system. It could reduce the so-called premium on housing near to what are currently considered good schools, and reduce the journey times to schools (since the nearest school would be as good as the furthest). All of this would be associated with a decline in socioeconomic and educational segregation between schools. Socioeconomic segregation (SES) between schools has been a rising problem in England since 1997 (Gorard 2009c). Reduced segregation by attainment and by pupil background has many advantages both for schools and for wider society, as well as becoming a repeating cycle, making schools genuinely comprehensive in intake as well as structure, so giving families even less reason to look beyond their nearest schools.

Perhaps even more importantly, once policy-makers understand how CVA works and that they cannot legitimately use it to differentiate school performance, they may begin to question the dominance of the school effectiveness model more generally. We might see a resurgence of political and research interest in school processes and outcomes other than pencil-and-paper test results. Schools are mini-societies in which pupils may learn how to interact, what to expect from wider society, and how to judge fairness (Gorard and Smith 2008). Schools seem to be a key influence on pupils' desire to take part in future learning opportunities (Gorard et al. 2007), and on their occupational aspirations (Gorard and Rees 2002). All of these outcomes have been largely ignored in three decades of school effectiveness research. It is time to move on. That is what we seek to do in this book.

Part II
Rethinking Equity in Education

3
Why Schools Might Matter

Introduction

As outlined at the start of Chapter 2, a growth in international comparative studies has led to considerable interest in isolating the desirable designed attributes of different school systems (McGaw 2008). The traditional approach to the design of school systems in developed countries tends to be based on a principle of educational effectiveness, seeking to improve standards of education as assessed by public test results, so leading to higher rankings in international comparative tests. Who goes to school with who is usually said to matter because there is generally believed to be a peer effect on attainment. A system of selective schools clusters the most able and least able pupils separately in order to provide learning and instruction at the most appropriate level for their different intakes. In addition, the mere act of attending school with others like them is meant to improve the attainment of pupils. This principle can lead to overtly selective systems, such as those in Germany or Austria, where pupils are allocated to schools on the basis of earlier attainment or purported talent. The idea is that each pupil is then taught with their similar peers, and provided with an appropriate education, such as academic, technical or vocational pathways. Another form of selection occurs indirectly where pupils are sorted into school by factors other than academic selection, such as religion, ability to pay, ability to travel, or neighbourhood (as they are in several of the countries involved in our new study – see Chapter 6).

However, the assumption that there is a peer effect on attainment has never been shown to be valid. It is highly questionable in principle (Gorard 2006b, Nash 2003), since there is just not enough variation between the schools in any national system to be accounted for by a peer effect. Schools differ in their academic outcomes (test scores) largely because they vary in their pupil intake. If the prior attainment and background characteristics of pupils are taken into account less than 20% of the variation in outcomes between schools remains (see Chapter 2). The residual so-called value-added scores must, by design, be at least 50% explicable by the raw-scores they are intended to replace – since they are simply the differences between two sets of raw-scores, each of which contributes exactly 50% to the variation in the result (Gorard 2008c). In fact, recent work has shown that between 60% and 90% of the residual 20% value-added score is still attributable to the raw-score outcomes of the school – that is, schools with high raw-scores tend to have high value-added scores as well (Gorard 2006a). If we work with a generous estimate of 40% of the 20% residual variation still not explained by raw-scores, then the *maximum* possible school effect is a mere 8%.

As Chapter 2 illustrates in detail, this 8% residual difference between school outcomes is almost entirely an error term stemming from initial measurement error and missing data. A true school effect can only be found in the fraction of that 8% left after accounting for error. This fraction of variation in pupil results that is potentially attributable to schools (and local authorities) is then fought over by various commentators, with different interests, like scraps from the table. Some analysts claim that leadership has an impact on school outcomes. Some would argue that differential school funding needs to be taken into account. Some would focus on the qualifications of the staff. Others would argue that an analysis at school level is misguided, and that it is subject departments and/or individual teachers that are key (Sanders and Horn 1998). A school peer effect, such that a pupil's school outcome was influenced by who else was at the school is just one more possible explanation for a sub-set *of* a fraction of 8% variation. There are just not enough scraps to go around.

Therefore, the pedagogic argument for segregation, that pupils make more progress when educated with those like them, is not sustained by the available evidence (Luyten et al. 2009). In fact, there is very little relationship between the abilities of school peers on entry to the school and the later examination outcomes of individuals (Gibbons and Telhaj 2006). And any small gain that did appear from a peer effect could be at least counter-balanced by the negative peer effect of placing low attainers in one group – making it zero-sum at best. The economic argument for pupil segregation, that concentrations of disadvantage permit effective targeting of resources, is also not borne out in practice – witness

Educational Action Zones, Excellence in Cities (Kendall et al. 2005), or (City) Academies in England (Gorard 2005, 2009d).

Internationally, repeated studies have shown no tension between equity of provision and quality (McGaw 2008). Some countries, such as those in Scandinavia, appear to have highly equitable school systems and high-quality school outcomes. Others, like Italy, have high equity and lower quality outcomes. The United Kingdom, France, and Belgium, for example, have reasonably high-quality outcomes but are lower in equity. And the Czech Republic seems to have relatively low equity and low quality. There is no clear pattern of relationship between test scores and segregation in PISA 2003 (Gorard 2007a). Countries like Greece and Portugal have high levels of segregation by parental occupation and low tests scores, with respective plausible values of only 441 and 446 in Maths. The 'plausible' values are an estimate of pupil attainment, having a standardised mean of 500. Finland has low segregation overall, and a plausible value of 543 in Maths. However, Belgium has a plausible value of 533 in Maths and high segregation by reading score and parental occupation, whereas Luxembourg has low segregation overall and a score of 494 in Maths. One conclusion is clear. There is no evidence of a sustained advantage from having a segregated system, in terms of results. But segregated systems could have some disadvantages that are not directly related to academic attainment, as the remainder of this chapter shows. Here we look at the variation in school mix in terms of creating a just environment for pupils.

The variation in school mix

Before looking at the possible costs or downside of separating different kinds of pupils in different schools, we first illustrate the range of pupil segregation that occurs in practice. 'Segregation' here refers to the unevenness of pupil allocation to schools in terms of their background characteristics. It is a measure of the extent to which poor, or otherwise disadvantaged, children are clustered in specific schools (Gorard and Taylor 2002). In a series of previous publications, we have illustrated clear differences between varying national systems of allocating pupils to secondary schools and the ensuing clustered nature of the intake to each school (EGREES 2005). All other things being equal, systems without tiering or selection by the schools have lower intake segregation (Gorard 2007b). The same thing applies to regions and local areas. In the United Kingdom, for example, local areas that retain selection to grammar schools have higher levels of pupil segregation by poverty than areas using non-selective systems (Gorard et al. 2003). The same applies to the clustering of pupils in specific schools by ethnicity, country of origin, first language, and specific learning difficulties. Diversity of school types is strongly associated with higher segregation of pupil intakes (Gorard et al. 2003, West and Hind 2006).

Using PISA 2000 figures for the 15 countries of the EU at the time, Table 3.1 shows how clustered the intakes to schools are in terms of three measures of relative disadvantage. In general, countries with selective school systems, whether by ability, ability to pay, or religious belief, have the most clustered schools in terms of reading scores. Austria, for example, had a tracked system in which 62% of the weakest readers would have to exchange schools for these to be evenly distributed between schools. Sweden, on the other hand, had a local comprehensive system of allocating school places, in which only 29% of the weakest readers would have to exchange schools for these to be evenly distributed between schools (Gorard and Smith 2004). In addition, figures for

Table 3.1 Segregation indices for the lowest 10% by reading score, parental occupation, and index of family wealth, and for pupils born outside their country of residence

Country	Reading score	Parental occupation	Country of origin
Belgium	66	36	45
Netherlands	66	30	41
Austria	62	36	49
Germany	61	36	41
Greece	58	43	48
Italy	58	30	55
France	56	31	47
Portugal	48	40	35
U.K.	43	31	46
Luxembourg	41	24	24
Spain	40	32	57
Denmark	39	33	42
Ireland	39	29	45
Sweden	29	27	40
Finland	27	36	55

Note: The values in each cell are 'Gorard' segregation indices calculated for the lowest 10% of the sample as measured by parental occupation or reading score, or for those born outside the test country. They are the percentage of the disadvantaged group that would have to exchange schools for there to be no clustering (see Gorard 2009c).

both PISA 2000 and 2003 show there is a strong link between clustering by ability/attainment in any country and clustering by social and ethnic background of the pupils in the same country (yielding Pearson correlations of over 0.6). For example, Sweden has one of the lowest scores for clustering by reading score, and also by parental occupation. Luxembourg has a low score for clustering on both measures, and for non-native pupils. Austria has high scores for clustering on all measures including the clustering of pupils born outside the country. There are even stronger links between various measures of SES such as parental qualification, parental years in schooling, socioeconomic and cultural status, occupational status, and blue/white collar classification, for all 41 countries (Gorard 2007a). Overall, the Scandinavian countries of Sweden, Finland and Denmark show less segregation on most indicators of pupil disadvantage, while Germany, Greece and Belgium show the most. Ranking the 27 European countries taking part in PISA 2003 in terms of the difference in Maths scores between native and non-native pupils shows Belgium, Netherlands, Portugal, and Germany having large gaps, and Ireland and the United Kingdom with much smaller gaps. Unsurprisingly, national and regional policies for allocating school places seem to make a difference to school intakes (Eurydice 2007a).

In general, attitudes to school are also somewhat worse in countries with segregated systems. The PISA 2003 scores for this construct (attitudes to school) are −.07 for Belgium, −.04 for Germany, −.08 for Greece, and −.07 for Netherlands. By way of comparison, they are almost neutral for Finland and Ireland (−.01), and a much higher +.21 for Sweden, and +.18 for the United Kingdom. A similar, but slightly weaker, pattern applies to the construct 'a sense of belonging to school'. The scores for Belgium are −.25, and for the Netherlands −.05. The scores for Sweden are +.26, and for the United Kingdom +.08. However, Austria breaks the pattern with a score of +.44 compared to 0 for Finland. Despite the incomplete nature of the pattern, there is enough evidence from the two PISA studies using these and other variables to suggest that segregated school systems could endanger pupils' attitudes to schools and sense of belonging, and for no clear gain in outcome scores (as shown in Chapter 2). The Netherlands has a gap of −19.5 for attitude to school between native and non-native pupils. Non-native pupils there report feeling very isolated (perhaps part of the explanation for their depressed outcome scores). The gap for Germany is −12, whereas for the less segregated Finland it is −.3, and for Luxembourg +1.3.

In our own prior work, involving a survey of 6000 school pupils in five EU countries, pupils in countries with more segregated systems tend to report greater favouritism for one or more groups of pupils (Smith and Gorard 2006). Often, it was the girls, the brighter children, and those from richer families, who were thought by other pupils to benefit from more favourable treatment. Pupils generally reported wanting an egalitarian system where all pupils were treated in the same way. In four countries a considerable number of pupils also thought that the least able should receive more support and attention in class. This view was particularly marked among pupils who reported achieving low marks. In the United Kingdom, the overwhelming majority believed that all pupils should receive the same attention. There was almost no support in any of the countries for the notion that able pupils should receive the most attention (Table 3.2).

Table 3.3 shows the same 6000 pupils' estimation of how equitable their education system actually is. The clear opinion across all countries and groups is that schools generally provide the same quality of education for all pupils (around 75% reported this in all countries). There is also some limited support, especially in France and Spain, for the idea that schools actually provide a better education for the most able. There is almost no support for the idea that schools are providing a better education for the least able. Therefore, all systems are seen to be failing to meet one specific demand for equity. Other than in the United Kingdom, there is considerable disparity between the proportion of pupils wanting a system in which less able pupils receive more attention (around 40%) and the proportion who experience this in their school. For example, in Italy, 46% of pupils felt that secondary schools should provide more attention to the least able pupils, whereas

Table 3.2   Percentage of pupils agreeing with statements about fair treatment, by country

For a secondary school to be fair, its teachers must give…	Belgium	Spain	France	Italy	United Kingdom
…the same attention to all pupils	54	65	59	53	81
…more attention to the most able	2	4	3	1	6
…more attention to the least able	44	31	38	46	13
Total	100	100	100	100	100

Note: The table shows the percentage of pupils who chose each statement as the closest to their view.
Source: Smith and Gorard (2006).

Table 3.3 Percentage of pupils agreeing with statements about national education, by country

In <country of test>, school offers...	Belgium	Spain	France	Italy	United Kingdom
...the best education for the most able	17	20	20	15	17
...the same quality of education for all	79	76	73	76	77
...the best education for the least able	4	4	7	10	6

Note: The table shows the percentage of pupils who chose each statement as the closest to their view.
Source: Smith and Gorard (2006).

Table 3.4 Pupils' perspectives on the treatment of different groups of pupils

In my school...	Belgium	Spain	France	Italy	United Kingdom
the teachers treat pupils who come from <country of test> better than those who have come from abroad	14	11	19	6	8
the teachers treat the most able pupils the best	42	49	56	34	38
the teachers treat the hard-working pupils the best	70	78	76	53	62

Note: The table shows the percentage of pupils who chose each statement as the closest to their view.
Source: Smith and Gorard (2006).

only 10% report that this was actually the case in their country. Conversely, only around 3% of pupils in France had reported wanting a system which gave more attention to the most able, whereas around 20% reported experiencing such a system. In the United Kingdom, most pupils want all pupils treated the same, and this is largely what they report experiencing. In France, Spain, Belgium and Italy, more pupils want greater attention for the least able but pupils in all countries also report actually experiencing somewhat greater attention for the most able.

Table 3.4 shows examples of some of the survey items about the treatment of these 6000 pupils in their schools. In general, again, pupils in countries with more segregated systems tend to report greater favouritism for one or more groups of pupils.

If this is pupils' experience of treatment at school, and if the pupils in the more segregated countries experience more unfairness, then what does this mean for their aspirations, participation and preparation as future citizens? These are the issues discussed in the next sections.

Aspirations and the school mix

Does the structure of national schooling and the associated sorting or mixing of pupils have an impact on pupil aspirations? In our prior studies aspiration for a professional/managerial occupation after school was found to be heavily influenced by pupil family background factors, in the same way as pupil attainment (see Chapter 2). Using a large dataset for England, Table 3.5 illustrates a logistic regression model distinguishing those 56% of pupils wanting a professional occupation from all others. This dataset is different from that presented in Chapters 7–10, and which forms the substance of this book, in that it is smaller, only involves pupils in England and because uncovering pupil sense of justice was not its primary aim. Our logistic regressions attempt to predict which pupils will present a particular outcome (such as wanting a professional occupation) using a range of possible predictor variables. The pupil background variables were entered in the first stage – such as sex and parental occupation – and explain 21% of the variation in responses. The school variables entered in the second stage – such as type of school and nature of its intake – explain a further 6%. The reported individual experiences of pupils at school explain about the same amount of variation again as the background. At each stage the new variables can only explain variation left over from the previous stages.

As might be expected, pupils whose parents are professional are more likely to want a professional occupation themselves. Also, males, those from families living in poverty or for whom English is a first language, and those with lower prior qualifications are less likely to want a professional occupation. Once these stratifying individual intake values are accounted for, there is still noticeable variation explicable at the school level (6% in Table 3.5). Thus, schools with high proportions of professional background pupils tend to have more pupils aspiring to a professional occupation, whatever their own background. Similarly, schools with a high proportion of pupils living in poverty tend to have pupils with lower professional aspirations. The school mix itself appears

Table 3.5 Accuracy of model for year 11 aspiration for professional occupation after education and training (N = 2,700)

Stage	Percentage of variation explained	Cumulative percentage explained
Pupil background variables	21	21
School-level variables	6	27
Individual experiences	22	49

Note: In this table, and others that follow, the figures show the percentage of variation in pupil responses that can be explained by each group of variables. For example, the pupil reports of experiences at school explain 22% of the variation in responses, over and above 21% explained by pupil background, and the 6% for school characteristics.
Source: Gorard et al. (2009a).

to be associated with providing possible futures for young people. This conclusion is backed up by other studies showing parental occupation and a peer effect as determinants of intention to remain in education after school-leaving age (Thomas and Webber 2009). We test this further with the much larger international dataset in Chapter 10.

The curriculum structure may also be relevant. Our research has shown that pupils following largely vocational programmes aspire to achieve vocational qualifications and enter skilled trades. In some cases they are planning to work with family or adult friends (Gorard et al. 2009a). However, in terms of equity, their perceived lack of professional ambition might also be judged as poverty of aspiration – a result of inequity of opportunity perhaps. It is a difficult judgement. Vocational courses have been presented as a way of adapting the traditional liberal curriculum to improve access to education and training for otherwise marginalised pupils. But, in Australia at least, such programmes have been reported as of poor quality, serving working-class pupils in deprived areas (Polesel 2008). Thus, providing an alternative even though it may be intended to have parity of esteem tends to make schools intakes and outcomes even more stratified by social class and ability.

The highest educational and occupational aspirations are sometimes reported by young people with the lowest levels of attainment, and so perhaps with the least realistic expectations of attaining these ambitions (Strand and Winston 2008). But pupils who are restricted in their choice of courses at age 14 by low prior attainment are generally less likely to want a professional occupation (Gorard et al. 2009a). This leads to a kind of education-based discrimination, which is too often overlooked (Tannock 2008). In most developed countries, and certainly in the EU, it is illegal to select people for occupations on the basis of age, sex, social class, ethnicity and so on. Yet we continue to select on the basis of academic attainment, despite knowing that attainment is clearly stratified by these same 'illegal' variables (Gorard et al. 2007). In many ways it makes no sense (Walford 2004).

Of course, these problems and their solutions are not just structural and curricular, as discussed further in the next chapter. The way in which pupils are treated by their teachers may also have a major influence on lowering aspirations:

> When I actually went for an interview at [agricultural college] and got my place ... I showed my Head of House and ... she actually turned round and said that it's a load of rubbish, there's no point doing it, 'cos I ain't going to get nowhere in life 'cos I never come to school ... I might as well just drop all my dreams and just be a bum, basically, live off Social. Which really put me down. (Pupil, in Gorard et al. 2009a)

> Every lesson 'you are all gonna fail' and then he might set you an assignment to write and he will say 'hand my at the end of' ... and then you are handing in your work 'so let's see what is worth laughing on this paper'. You do not want to hear that you have done your best you expect a teacher to behave like a teacher and not criticize you and tell you that 'you are gonna fail'. (Pupil, in Gorard et al. 2009a)

Participation and the school mix

Linked to aspiration are the actual patterns of educational participation for pupils once they reach the official school-leaving age in any country. As with attainment and aspiration, post-compulsory education is stratified by socioeconomic origin (Gorard and See 2009). Previous research has shown that participation in education for young people aged from 14 onwards becomes increasingly stratified by pupil background and everything associated with that, such as higher average levels of prior attainment (Gorard et al. 2007). And this pattern continues lifelong, with around one-third of adults in England never again participating in any kind of formal education or training, nor reporting a pastime or hobby requiring them to learn informally (Macleod and Lambe 2008, Selwyn et al. 2006). There is increasing evidence that despite the stratification of this pattern – non-participants are generally less qualified, from less educated and lower occupational status families, and so on – schools have a role in reinforcing or weakening it.

Using the same England-based study as in the previous section, 55% of year 11 pupils in England reported planning to continue in education at age 16 (a similar picture emerges from the study at OFSTED 2007, with 50% of years 6 to 10 wanting to study to HE level after school). This is a low figure, and since these data were recorded the government has announced plans for all young people in England to remain in education or training until after age 17. Table 3.6 is like Table 3.5, but this time illustrating a logistic regression model distinguishing those pupils wanting to stay on in education after the age of 16 from all others. Pupils from professional backgrounds, those not eligible for free school meals, and girls, are more likely to report being encouraged to learn, and to want to continue at age 16. Once such pupil background is accounted for, those at independent schools report more encouragement to learn, and desire to continue post-16, followed by those at schools in charge of their own admissions, then those at local authority comprehensives. However, it seems that different kinds of schools are not particularly different in encouraging pupils to continue in education, except via their intake. Although the impact is small, there is an intake mix 'effect', as with aspiration (see above).

A major influence on pupil *a priori* interest in continuing in education comes from their reports of experiences of education so far – especially

Table 3.6   Accuracy of model for year 11 pupils planning to continue in education (N = 2,700)

Stage	Percentage of variation explained	Cumulative percentage explained
Pupil background variables	30	30
School-level variables	4	34
Individual experiences	20	54

Source: Gorard et al. (2009a).

encouragement to think for themselves and the quality of guidance on offer. Feeling encouraged to learn more and intending to continue at age 16 are both associated with the quality of guidance for the future, pupil autonomy in setting learning targets, and being encouraged by teachers to make up their own minds. In addition, experience of contact with pupils on other programmes, or of learning delivered at college (while attending school) or in a work environment, is associated with continuation in education at the next key moment. Sometimes the impact of treating the pupils differently and in a more adult way is even greater off-site, when they are deemed to have 'failed' at school. According to one adult:

> We find that, it never ceases to amaze me, they are completely different creatures down at [project name]. I've heard, I think, one young lady, she came from [school name] and apparently from all accounts, she was a bit of a horror, you know, and she's absolutely perfect at [project name]. She behaves herself. She does as she's asked. And when you ask her why, she says it's the way she's spoken to. She feels that sometimes teachers don't speak to her with the respect that she deserves. (Employer, in Gorard et al. 2009a)

Our pupil accounts strongly suggest that some differences could be based on a feeling of being treated more as a young adult in some institutions – a notably less common occurrence in schools under local authority control. For example, a pupil in a comprehensive school says:

> Some teachers don't respect you and wonder why you cause so much trouble...The teachers say we want respect from you but they don't normally show it to us. They're the teacher they're always right, we're the kid and we don't know what we are going on about. (Pupil, in Gorard et al. 2009a)

Those learning partly at college (while attending school) or in a work environment are more likely to want to continue in education at age 16 than equivalent pupils remaining solely in school. This could be as much a consequence of who chooses (or is chosen) to have learning delivered off-site as a consequence of that learning itself. But again it could be a consequence of how they are treated by adults in these different settings. Perhaps a key possible explanatory variable here that links to the mix effect is pupils reporting contact with pupils on other courses or programmes (perhaps via vertical programmes and activities or simply because of a small institution). These are more likely to want to continue in education. One reason could be that they become aware of the range of possibilities. If so, this is another reason for mixing pupils of different types within as well as between schools.

However, all of these results are about intention to continue in education. Other work by us has suggested that while the treatment of pupils at school might influence reported intentions, the actual decision to continue or not (as revealed *a posteriori*) is more influenced by who the pupil goes to school with, and the structure and organisation of the school. For example, relatively high-attaining pupils in low-attaining schools (on average) are more likely to continue in education post-16 (a big fish effect perhaps) even where their attainment is lower than relatively low-attaining pupils in high-attaining schools (Lumby et al. 2004). Pupils in schools that range in age from 11 to 16 are anyway less likely to continue post-16 (elsewhere) than pupils in schools running from age 11 to 18 – perhaps because more of them have to make an explicit decision (Lumby et al. 2006). So, it is the combination of the structure and the intake of schools with the treatment of pupils within them, that could influence pupils' futures.

Discussion

In our prior studies, once the 'influence' of individual pupil background variables is accounted for, a smaller but still noteworthy proportion of variation in pupil outcomes is accounted for by the same variables aggregated to school level, and in the same direction as above. For example, the proportion of professional and managerial parents is positively related to the professional aspiration of pupils, regardless of the occupation of their own parents. This may be evidence of a kind of school mix effect. Whatever the causal model is, parental occupation and all that may stem from that is a key determinant of achievement, participation, enjoyment and citizenship. This is an issue going well beyond education, affecting all public services. Schools and school systems with pupil intakes that are mixed in terms of parental occupation perform at least as well as segregated schools while apparently raising aspirations for education and occupation. Peer group interaction in settings with high proportions of less aspirational or low-attaining pupils can actually worsen anti-school and anti-society behaviour (Kelly 2009).

The school mix therefore appears to matter because it provides the context for creating pupils' awareness of equity and of their future opportunities in society (Halstead and Taylor 2000, Meuret 2001). Mainstream schooling has a generally positive effect on aspirations of pupils with learning difficulties, for example (Casey et al. 2006), and so acts as a determinant of their lifelong aspirations (Gorard and Rees 2002). The school mix of pupils can affect attitudes, outcomes and patterns of residential integration (Burgess et al. 2005). For those below average attainment, attending selective schools appears to negatively affect their academic self-concept, and this is a reasonably long-lasting effect (Marsh et al. 2007). Tracking from an early age can also have a dispiriting effect on the lifelong aspirations of the majority (Casey et al. 2006, Gorard and Rees 2002). Inclusive schools are generally more tolerant (Slee 2001), and exhibit that tolerance in racial, social and religious terms, and this is also associated with greater civic awareness (Schagen 2002).

People growing up in segregated settings generally receive poorer instruction, fewer local services, substandard materials, less able teachers, more dilapidated plant, and face higher crime, and greater poverty. So they may grow up less prepared for the academic challenges of post-school education. They may be socially unprepared to face diversity, feel that they do not belong in a mixed society, and this can inhibit their performance. This is partly because social and ethnic segregation is usually also linked to poverty and everything that is associated with it, such as health and delinquency (Massey and Fischer 2006). The level of ethnic, and other, segregation between schools can affect racial attitudes, subsequent social and economic outcomes, and patterns of residential segregation (Clotfelter 2001). For those not speaking the language of their country of residence, the most important factor in successful learning was exposure to native speakers (Lee and Madyun 2008).

Increasing the number of faith-based schools through conversion of secular schools, growth of Muslim provision and creationist academies in England, for example, can turn schools into forces for even greater societal segregation (Grayling 2005, Smith 2003), with teachers unwilling even to discuss issues of sectarianism with their (segregated) pupils (Mansell 2005). So, in divided societies, citizenship education can actually generate negative results, including the ghettoisation of minority communities, perhaps culminating in greater social unrest as it has in some central European countries (Print and Coleman 2003). Institutional differentiation is associated with a greater influence of SES background on attainment. The number of distinct school types and programmes in any country is correlated with the apparent significance of SES for pupil outcomes, and with reportedly lower levels of support from teachers for those most in need. Thus, integrated, rather than selective or tracked, school systems seem to lead to the desirable outcome that a pupil's achievement depends less on their social and cultural background (Dupriez and Dumay 2006, Schutz et al. 2008). Although most egalitarian school systems are also set in countries with egalitarian structures and income equality anyway, these systems are designed to delay for as long as possible the separation of pupils by attainment (Boudon 1973). This allows most time for schools to counteract resource differences between pupil families.

One of the purposes of compulsory education in developed countries is to try and compensate for early disadvantage. But quality and equality are not mutually exclusive – in fact the most successful countries in international tests tend to have the lowest social gradient – that is the smallest difference in test scores attributable to socioeconomic variables – and the lowest levels of socioeconomic segregation between schools (Haahr et al. 2005, Marks et al. 2006). This finding, in turn, suggests that policy-makers have an opportunity to revise their traditional and long-held principles when organising and seeking to improve school systems. We revisit this, as we consider the impact of the treatment of pupils at school in the next chapter.

4
Why Teachers Might Matter

Introduction

Following on from consideration of the possible impact of school intakes and structures on pupil aspiration and future educational participation, this chapter focuses more on social interactions within schools. Issues of equity arise in the way pupils interact with teachers and other pupils. We look at pupils' experiences of school in terms of their enjoyment of learning and behaviour, and consider their preparation for roles as active citizens. We present existing evidence from the literature, and from a large mixed dataset generated by our own previous research, as described in Chapter 3. Of course, the structure and intakes of schools as discussed in Chapter 3 are probably linked to the experiences of pupils in those schools as described here. So the evidence in this chapter differs largely in emphasis rather than substance from the kind of evidence in the last chapter.

Experience of school

The dataset from our previous work, described in Chapter 3, suggests that a majority of pupils nearing the end of their compulsory schooling do not enjoy education (Table 4.1). A clear majority report that lessons are uninteresting.

Similar conclusions have been drawn from school inspections in England, where OFSTED reports that teaching is too often boring and uninspiring (Marley 2009). OFSTED (2007) also found that 30% of pupils had been bullied at school in the prior four weeks, and 5% were bullied on most days. The most popular suggestion to improve schools

Table 4.1   Percentage of year 11 pupils agreeing with each statement about enjoyment (N = 2,700)

Most lessons are interesting	38
I enjoy school/college	44

Source: Gorard et al. (2009a).

Table 4.2   Accuracy of model for predicting responses to 'Most lessons are interesting' (N = 2,700)

Stage	Percentage of variation explained	Cumulative percentage explained
Pupil background	4	4
School characteristics	0	4
Individual pupil experience	38	42

Note: In this table, and others that follow, the figures show the percentage of variation in pupil responses that can be explained by each group of variables. For example, the pupil reports of experiences at school explain 38% of the variation in responses, over and above 4% explained by pupil background. School characteristics add nothing to the accuracy of the explanation.
Source: Gorard et al. (2009a).

from the pupils in that study (79%), however, was to make the lessons more interesting and enjoyable.

Almost none of the variation in responses about whether lessons are interesting is explicable by the pupil intake to schools or other school-level factors (unlike the models in the final sections of Chapter 3). Reports of interest and enjoyment are not stratified by the standard sociological variables of class, sex, ethnicity and so on. It is the experience of individual pupils in schools that is our key to understanding interest and enjoyment of education (Table 4.2).

Predictably, perhaps, pupils report finding lessons more interesting when they feel in control of choosing their subjects of study (relatively unconstrained by curriculum and timetable, and with appropriate information or guidance), when the classes are small, and the teachers appear to have the appropriate specialist knowledge. Learners generally want variety of delivery to include discussion, field visits, contact with pupils on other programmes, and practical work. Above all, they want some feeling of control over their own learning in terms of the pace at which they proceed and the way in which they make decisions about evidence or sources of information. These factors together explain over 40% of the variation in reporting finding school lessons interesting. The situation for 'enjoyment of school' is very similar, mostly involving individually reported issues at school such as appropriate autonomy and variety. Of course, enjoyment of school encompasses more than the lessons. Pupils often mentioned the social aspects of school, like making friends, as reasons for going to school. But the modal response was an appreciation of innovation, preparation and variety in learning activities. For example:

> Like in English one time, we were doing poetry and we had a poem, and we had to do freeze frames for it, like for the poem. And we got to dress up and then we had to do a freeze frame to represent the whole poem, which was good. So you understood how people were feeling, like they might have been feeling in that poem and how they might have stood and things. (Pupil, in Gorard et al. 2009a)

The experiences which were widely perceived to undermine enjoyment were passive pedagogy, such as listening to a teacher for lengthy periods, copying, note taking, and having to sit still for a prolonged period. Many pupils did not like the classic style of lesson:

> He just stands at the blackboard, or the whiteboard...and just writing on the board... (Pupil, in Gorard et al. 2009a)

The connection between active learning and enjoyment and passive learning and lack of enjoyment was widely made by pupils. It is surprising that lessons for year 11 pupils still consist of so much 'chalk and talk'. Teaching was seen by many as unsatisfactory. Perceptions included that pupils were left without help:

> [The teacher will] give you a sheet and you'll just go through each question and they might not even, unless you express a want to be told how to do it, they might not even, you know, support you in any way. (Pupil, in Gorard et al. 2009a)

Asked to engage in meaningless activities:

> We're given a sheet and we're just spoken to and we write down notes and then the sheet is, at the end of the hour, two-hour lesson, is

lost and never seen again. We don't really learn that way. (Pupil, in Gorard et al. 2009a)

And alienated by repetition and boredom:

> I don't think there's many teachers in this school that understand that like kids learn in different ways. (Pupil, in Gorard 2009a)

> There is never really a surprise when you go into a lesson. (Pupil, in Gorard et al. 2009a)

It was more motivating for pupils like the following to be able to discuss things in class:

> Like, sometimes, teachers think it's a good idea for you to sit silently in class, and to only listen to them...but I think it's good for to be able to talk between yourselves and...not, like, obviously about the subject. But to be able to sit there in silence for an hour lesson just looking at a whiteboard, it does give you a headache. (Pupil, in Gorard et al. 2009a)

Or even better to use a less traditional method such as peer-teaching:

> And sometimes they get us to do presentations, like us teaching the class so it sort of helps us to learn it as well...so it can be boring...sitting there with a teacher and we just switch off so she gets us to actively teach the other person so that get us to know the textbook as well. (Pupil, in Gorard et al. 2009a)

Or role-playing:

> We had to do this electrons thing and then the teacher got us all to stand round in a circle and we had to hold this rope, and we were the electrons and then we kind of moved around, so they only move in one way the electrons. If like one falls, then the other can like push the other one. (Pupil, in Gorard et al. 2009a)

In general, the pupils in this study held relatively negative views about the teaching and learning experience in their schools. In the following section we consider how these experiences may relate to the role of the school in preparing students to be active citizens.

Preparation for citizenship

From 1996, the Council of Europe expressed concern over the dangers of intolerance within each country towards elements of society deemed different, such as recent immigrants and local ethnic minorities. This concern was one part of the drive towards the establishment of the Crick committee in the United Kingdom that would, in turn, lead to the compulsory National Curriculum for citizenship in England (Davies et al. 2005). Citizenship education has been presented by government as the means by which societal problems can be ameliorated, because it has important implications for developing pupils' perceptions about what it is to be part of an equitable and democratic society. The teaching of citizenship and democracy is, purportedly, needed to counter 'worrying levels of apathy, ignorance and cynicism about public life' (QCA 1998, p. 8). The model for citizenship teaching has, at its foundation, a curriculum based around the key concepts of 'fairness, rights and responsibilities', which seeks to encourage in pupils 'self-confidence and socially and morally responsible behaviour both in and beyond the classroom, towards those in authority and towards each other' (DfES 2002, p. 20), to such an extent as to cause 'no less than a change in the political culture of this country both nationally and locally' (QCA 1998, p. 7). Of course, citizenship is a disputed concept, and influential bodies such as OECD propose a 'very particular liberal and individualised conception of a worthy citizen, who is created through lifelong learning' (Walker 2009, p. 348).

Close to the heart of developing a model of democratic citizenship among pupils is the need to encourage children to develop their own concepts of fairness, and probably the fundamental influence on pupils in developing their perceptions of what constitutes a fair and equitable society is their experience of school (Davies and Evans 2002, Howard and Gill 2000, Wilson 1959).

Only a minority of year 11 pupils in Gorard et al. (2009a) reported having participated, or even intending to participate, in the kinds of activities considered to promote active citizenship (Table 4.3). These figures for participation in a school election are even lower than those reported to OFSTED (2007) by younger children ranging from year 6 to year 10, of whom 43% voted in one school year. The figures for charity assistance are much lower here than in the OFSTED study, which found 65% of pupils had helped raise money for charity in one school year. Part of the difference could be age, in that primary schools where many of the OFSTED respondents were based may be more active in

Table 4.3 Percentage of year 11 pupils agreeing with each statement about citizenship (N = 2,700)

Volunteered to help charity or local organisation	25
Voted in school/college elections	38
Would vote in election this week	44

Source: Gorard et al. (2009a).

Table 4.4 Accuracy of model for 'voted in school elections' (N = 2,700)

Stage	Percentage of variation explained	Cumulative percentage explained
Pupil background variables	12	12
School-level variables	8	20
Individual experiences	27	47

Source: Gorard et al. (2009a).

charity collections involving all pupils. But most of the difference could be that the OFSTED focus was on what took place at school, whereas our focus was intended to be on out-of-school activities (voluntary) for two of the questions.

The possible 'determinants' of citizenship participation in the form of voting in school/college elections include pupil and school characteristics to some extent (Table 4.4). The pattern for other citizen activity is similar. Pupils from families with a mother and/or father in a professional occupation are more likely to report voting in school/college elections, and all other examples of citizenship activity (see also Paterson 2009). Of more interest perhaps is the lack of association with many other pupil background variables, such as poverty, ethnicity, language, immigration, and so on. The stratification only relates to parental occupation. In schools where the staff report focusing on trying to raise aspirations, the pupils report more citizenship activity. The individual pupil experiences positively associated with voting and charitable behaviour are very similar to those for enjoyment of school. These include autonomy in learning, individual attention from teachers, and having contact with pupils on other programmes or via work experience.

A much higher proportion of pupils suggest that they feel ready for work, and for handling issues that will arise in their future lives (Table 4.5). One might be tempted to dismiss this high level of preparedness as 'bravado' on the part of pupils if it were not for the clear differences in this preparedness for pupils with different individual experiences of the quality of education (see below).

Almost none of the variation in pupil preparedness for future life is related to their background or to school-level factors (Table 4.6). Similarly, very little of the variation in responses to questions about preparedness for handling health, relationships, or money is explicable by pupil background or school-level factors. Basically, the same proportion of pupils of all kinds, on any course, at all types of institutions, report being prepared to handle their work, relationships, finance and health. Nevertheless, the explanatory model here is a good one explaining nearly 50% of the variation, based on individual experiences of education.

There is some similarity to the determinants of civic participation, which is also substantially determined by pupil experiences at school. Pupils already involved in learning delivered at work, and those given good employment guidance, report being more prepared for the world

Table 4.5 Percentage of year 11 pupils agreeing with each statement about their future (N = 2,700)

Prepared for world of work	58
Prepared for future relationships	67
Prepared to handle my own money	70
Prepared to handle my own health	78

Source: Gorard et al. (2009a).

Table 4.6 Accuracy of model for 'prepared for world of work' (N = 2,700)

Stage	Percentage of variation explained	Cumulative percentage explained
Pupil background variables	3	3
School-level variables	4	7
Individual experiences	42	49

Source: Gorard et al. (2009a).

of work – possibly because their exposure demonstrates the demands of work or because different kinds of pupils are currently learning at work. Pupils also feel better prepared when they have had enough chance to discuss issues in small enough groups. It is possible, of course, that factors such as these are a disguised intake effect such that schools with smaller classes are different in kind and in pupil intake from those with large classes, although the way in the models were constructed in stages protects against this to some extent (see Gorard et al. 2009b).

Discussion

It seems that pupil experiences and their interactions with teachers do influence outcomes such as aspiration and readiness for the future. What happens in school can impact on life outside and beyond school (Pugh and Bergin 2005). We therefore need to ask pupils about these experiences and their impact. Injustice and negative experiences at school *could* have positive effects such as greater autonomy and critical attitude on the part of pupils, or more effort in order to obtain fairer treatment (Dubet 1999). However, the negative effects are likely to be more important (Gilles 2004, Lerner 1980). These might include distress, insecurity, lower self-esteem and also consumption of energy, which can result in decreasing motivation, less hard work, less commitment in learning, and even in revolt, disruptive or violent behaviour, decreasing achievement, and sometimes also grade repetition in countries like France and Belgium, and dropping-out of school. Such effects can spill out over the entire class (or school) and the consequent deterioration of the social climate can result in decreasing achievement not only at an individual but also at the collective level. In addition, people with negative experiences during their initial education are less likely to participate in further educational experiences as adults (Gorard and Rees 2002). Experiencing serious injustices in school could undermine pupils' interpersonal and institutional trust, leading them to doubt that a just world is possible, and also encouraging passive attitudes towards political participation, membership in associations and so on. It could also favour the emergence of suspicious, aggressive, and intolerant attitudes towards others, particularly 'different' others such as recent immigrants.

In our new international study reported from here on, it was therefore our aim to obtain pupil perspectives on their experiences of fair and respectful treatment in school, their views on what fair schools should ideally be like, and their views on opportunities for equal participation in arrangements in and outside school. Further, we are concerned to explore how pupils' experiences of, and views on, equity and injustice in schools may be associated with their views on equity in wider society. The focus of the present study is thus to use pupil voice to 'hear' what pupils say about fairness and justice, in relation to school, learning, performance, and social relations. This is done with a view to exploring how these experiences may shape their trajectories in, and views on wider society. We are interested to examine how schools function as democratic institutions to instil a sense of equality, respect, and autonomy in pupils, and how/if is this reflected in their actual participation and views on society.

The next chapter looks at the importance of giving pupils a chance to discuss these issues, and how we achieved this in our new study.

Part III
Listening to Pupils

5
The Importance of Listening to Pupils

Introduction

This chapter summarises our reasons for listening to the views of pupils, illustrates what we mean by equity as the principle of fairness, and describes the underlying criteria that we use for understanding fairness. This then leads us to introduce the instrument that was developed to try and capture pupil views on equity. Chapter 6 will then look at the settings and the sample for our new work.

Schools are not generally structured, nor pupil places allocated, on the basis of fairness alone. Thus, pupils can experience dissonance between what they are being told and the way they live their lives in school. And inevitably, perhaps, some pupils report being treated unfairly – including being despised and humiliated by their teachers (Dubet 1999, Merle 2005). Across school systems, we know that some pupils are treated unfairly by some teachers, and that this has been the case for some time (Sirota 1988, Spender 1982).

These pupils' feelings of injustice matter. They matter for moral reasons, because there is an implicit promise in the basic conception of the modern educational system that every pupil's development and achievement is equally important for the system and for staff. Pupils' feelings may matter for academic reasons, because unfairly treated pupils are likely to react in a way that will impair their learning process and, more generally, pupils in classes and schools where a lot of injustice exists are likely to learn less well. These feelings matter for educational reasons, because unfairness may harm the personal development of pupils (lowering self-esteem, for instance). They matter for civic reasons, because unfairly treated pupils may develop inadequate conceptions of justice and other attitudes or beliefs detrimental to social cohesion and participation in active democracy. These feelings are probably even more important for disadvantaged pupils, as there is evidence that the opinions of teachers matter more to them than to other pupils (Meuret and Marivain 1997). And we have some evidence from PISA 2000/03 that low achievers and pupils from very socially disadvantaged backgrounds feel more injustice from their teachers than other pupils do (Meuret and Desvignes 2005). Thus, our aim is to investigate to what extent pupils do experience unfairness during compulsory schooling, and to what extent this can be detrimental to their education and later life, especially for disadvantaged pupils.

A more general concern of the present study was to identify the criteria that young people employ to describe fairness, or justice, and whether these principles are situational, or remain static across situations. We have previously established that school pupils seem to have a clear notion about what constitutes a fair and equitable national education system, and there is some evidence that this notion varies by country and place (EGREES 2005). What we examine in the evidence that follows in this book is whether pupils' sense of social justice is related to the mix of pupils they encounter and their experiences of schooling, and interactions with teachers.

In light of an emerging focus on the participatory potential of citizenship education, and the interest in viewing schools as micro-societies, an attempt was also made to explore how pupils' schooling experiences may shape their universal concepts of fairness and equity, in school as well as in wider society. This is particularly pertinent for pupils who are disadvantaged by virtue of physical or emotional difficulties, as well as pupils who belong to 'negatively labelled' groups, such as lower socioeconomic groups, minority ethnic groups, or sexual/religious minorities (Rose and Shevlin 2004). Research with excluded and disaffected (but still in mainstream schooling) pupils indicates particularly for older pupils that being treated with respect, being given some autonomy and being cared about as individuals by teachers is of great importance to them in relation to their self-worth/concept, as well as their willingness to learn (Riley 2004, Whitehead and Clough 2004). It is plausible that a self-concept as unsuccessful or incapable or unworthy of respect may influence a young person's sense of justice, their aspirations and potential for equal participation outside as well as within a learning environment. How did we find out?

The relevance of pupil voice

Over the last two decades or so, the right of young people to be actively engaged in the matters which concern them has become an important issue for policy-makers and legislators. For example, in England, the Every Child Matters agenda, emerging from the Children Act of 2004 – http://www.everychildmatters.gov.uk/participation/ – proposes a number of outcomes for all pupils, including being healthy and safe, making a positive contribution to society, and achieving economic well-being. The Qualifications and Curriculum Authority (QCA, see Chapter 2) introduced the 14–19 Reform Programme in September 2008. Among its objectives is the preparation of confident and responsible citizens. The introduction of citizenship education into the National Curriculum for England in 2002 brought attention to the potential of pupil voice in contributing to learning processes, and stimulated debate about the links between pupils' experiences of fairness, democracy, and participation in school and their views and expectations as citizens in society (DfES 2002). This complements a duty introduced under the 2002 Education Act, following the Childrens' Act 1989, that local authorities and school governing bodies must have regard to central guidance on consultation with *pupils* over matters affecting them, guidance which 'must provide for a pupil's views to be considered in the light of his or her age or understanding'. At time of writing, the U.K. government has also recently backed laws making it a requirement for schools to consult pupils on every aspect of their education from teaching to uniform (Stewart 2008); school governing bodies, for example, must now 'invite and consider pupil's views'. Several teacher organisations have objected to this new legislation, claiming that consultation works where it is done because it is appropriate not because it is legally enforced. However, the United Nations Convention of the Rights of the Child – http://www.therightssite.org.uk – has been ratified in the United Kingdom since 1991, and makes it clear that children have the right to say what they think should happen when adults are making decisions affecting them. This applies to schools and colleges as well as to families and wider society.

One of the ways that legislation and government guidance has envisaged these rights for children being embodied is through elected schools councils, which are deemed representative of pupil bodies. The National Curriculum for Personal, Social and Health Education (PSHE) and for Citizenship regards school councils as central to a school-wide approach – http://www.standards.dfes.gov.uk. Every Child Matters considers the percentage of children participating in the election of school council representatives as an important indicator of success. Indeed, school councils are now, reportedly, consulted during statutory inspections, and are used as an outlet for feeding back the results of inspection to all pupils – http://www.ofsted.gov.uk/.

It is not sufficient that children have these rights as pupils. Small-scale studies suggest that citizenship has to be fully integrated into the working of the school (as opposed to treated as merely a curriculum subject) if children are to become aware of these rights, and the responsibilities that accompany them (Cowell et al. 2008). As shown in the last two chapters, there is a reasonable body of evidence to suggest that school and experience at school, as well as family background, is related to the formation of social attitudes and participation in civic activities (Gorard and Smith 2008, Paterson 2009).

To understand more about equity in education, it is important to ask the participants themselves. The views of pupils are still surprisingly scarce in education research, despite pupils' clear competence as commentators (Wood 2003). The 1989 United Nations Convention on the Rights of the Child (see above) calls upon governments and agencies working with young people to acknowledge and act upon the views expressed in relation to decisions which directly affect their lives. Therefore, as education concerns its pupils, so they should be consulted seriously about its conduct and reform (Fielding and Bragg 2003), and treated with respect in its implementation (Osler 2000).

This is not something that is worth doing half-heartedly. In health studies, by way of analogy, it has been found that talking and teaching about healthy eating for pupils is largely ineffective unless the school also adopts a health-promoting whole-school approach, most obviously in its catering, but also by listening to and incorporating pupils' opinions/views on food, bodies and health (Christensen 2004). In the same way, pupil participation in citizenship may be best 'taught' by engaging pupils as active partners in school processes and not merely by its inclusion in the curriculum. This means moving away from a situation in which pupils largely experience schooling as something that is done to them, and in which they simply learn to perform in order to succeed (Duffield et al. 2000). If citizenship studies is to promote a climate of tolerance, democratic dialogue, respect for human rights and cultural diversity (Osler and Starkey 2006), then these characteristics can be made manifest in the structure and organisation of the school. Schools that model democratic values by promoting an open climate for discussion are more likely to be effective in promoting both civic knowledge and civic engagement among their pupils (Civic Education Study 2001, Torney-Purta et al. 2001).

Unfortunately, despite increasing prominence being given to pupil voice in official circles (such as the inspection system in England) and by schools, the extent to which pupils' views are listened to and used in genuinely democratic processes over which pupils can claim ownership are often 'compromised by political structures determined by adults' (Wyness 2006, p. 209). While pupils are the intended beneficiaries of much school and teaching reform, little evidence exists on their view of any of these initiatives (Duffield et al. 2000), primarily because they are often the object of research, and less often treated as key informants despite their clear competence as commentators (Whitehead and Clough 2004, Wood 2003). And, in many cases, the covert purpose of engaging with pupils like this is to increase pupil performance and attainment in academic terms (Noyes 2005), or to improve pupil self-confidence (Rose et al. 1999), rather than out of genuine interest in their views.

Some interest has been expressed in how pupil voice can be utilised to raise pupils' attainment and school performance. For example, Rose et al. (1999) found in their research among young people with learning difficulties, that the opportunity to give their views raised pupil self-awareness and that staff gained increased understanding of pupil needs and were more focused on actually addressing them through reformed pedagogical practices. But teachers are not always open to the opinions or suggestions for improvement that are voiced by pupils (Davie and Galloway 1996). As McIntyre et al. (2005, p. 150) point out, '[i]t cannot tenably be claimed that schooling is primarily intended to benefit pupils if pupils' own views about what is beneficial to them are not actively sought and attended to.'

There is little sense then from this literature as a whole that pupils might actually have sound views on equity and fairness in school processes, and that listening to them should be an aspect of democratic schooling that seeks to shape well-informed and critical citizens. Further, that engaging with pupil views could not only lead to real educational reform (Pomeroy 1999), but may have longer-term implications for young people's self-perceived capabilities, resources and values as citizens. The actual impact of suggestions or decisions made by pupil groups is often very limited (TES 2006). While participatory and democratic initiatives such as school councils are now widespread, a limited and highly selected proportion of pupils actually tend to be involved – certainly in England (Wyness 2006). There is little progress in terms of giving pupils a democratic say in the way their schools are run, or in facilitating their participation in, and contribution to, their local community.

Citizenship education in its current form may do 'little to challenge the anti-democratic nature of compulsory schooling, reinforcing the view that children and young people are citizens-in-the-making rather than citizens in their own right' (Wyness 2006, p. 210). It is no surprise, therefore, to find claims that the (arguably) 'original' aim of pupil voice research – to empower pupils and give them greater agency in their learning by establishing them as active agents in a democratic partnership – has been overlooked by some (Noyes 2005). It is the latter that could be thought to be particularly important for disadvantaged or marginalised pupils, if we are to understand and impact upon the way in which their experiences of school shape their views of wider society and hence, their potential, roles and trajectories as citizens in democratic society. While many pupils, including those who are marginalised or excluded, articulate that they are interested in learning and doing well at school (Riley 2004, Rose and Shevlin 2004), the issues of interest to them may be very different from those advanced by the teachers (Duffield et al. 2000, Hamill and Boyd 2002, McBeath et al. 2003).

It is important to note that the 'top' pupils, the most articulate and resourceful young people are usually those whose opinions are represented in research, those whose voices are most clearly heard. If researchers neglect to consider specifically the views of disadvantaged pupils or even middle-of-the-road pupils, then the use of pupil voice to effectuate change and increase participation might in fact, serve to reinforce existing hierarchies (see Reay 2006), in which the views of the disadvantaged and marginalised pupils are ignored or overlooked and the needs of the relatively most advantaged pupils are met.

The absence of voice is perhaps particularly marked for pupils in already marginalised groups. The skewed representation of pupils in the literature towards those already possessing advantages may lead to the 'uncritical adoption' of their partial view as an accurate reflection of all pupils' experiences and views of schooling and justice in school (Noyes 2005, p. 537). The pupil voice agenda may indeed support and reinforce those school structures which 'cause many children to develop a 'failing' identity' (Somekh 2001, p. 163) in school and in later life. It has become almost accepted that education research is about the educated, and participation studies are about those participating in education. Those currently marginalised in education are therefore also routinely excluded from research, even when that research is ostensibly about why they are excluded (Gorard et al. 2007). Thus, it is important in understanding more about equity to seek out the views of all, including the most disadvantaged and least likely to speak out.

What is equity?

'Equity' in the sense used in this book can represent two related ideas. First, equity is used as a synonym for the terms 'fair' and 'fairness'. It simply means the state, quality, or ideal of being impartial, just, and fair. Second, and more importantly, it refers to an attempt to understand how and why we can judge something to be fair or unfair. Of course, there are well-known principles, such as equality of treatment and equal access to opportunities, that purport to lay down what is fair. But there is no single principle or set of criteria that adheres in all situations. What then underlies our sense of whether a principle, such as equality of treatment, should be applied in a specific situation? Whatever that is, it is what we mean by equity in this second sense. The same situation applies in law, especially in a common-law system such as that in the United Kingdom, where the application of previous case law or strict adherence to legislation might give the plaintiff inadequate redress under certain conditions. So equity is like the underlying system of jurisprudence used to supplement and modify common law, where needed, to try and ensure that any outcome is truly fair (Gorard 2008d).

Without wishing to labour the point, it is important to be clear from the outset that any single formal criterion intended to enhance justice will be flawed in the sense that it will tend to lead to injustice in some situations (or at least it may lead to no improvement in justice, e.g., Themelis 2008). For example, should schools and teachers discriminate between pupils? We would probably not want schools to use more funds to educate boys than girls, or offer different curriculum subjects to different ethnic groups. But we might want schools to use more funds for pupils with learning difficulties, or to respect the right of each pupil to study their first language. Should a teacher be allowed to punish a pupil who misbehaves, or reward a pupil who has shown talent or effort? If so, then the teacher is being discriminating. If we adhere inflexibly to a principle of equality of opportunity, then the likely result in education will be marked inequality of outcomes. Is this acceptable? Those who start with greater talent, who can marshal greater resources at home, are the most interested in education, or who put the most effort into their study will tend to be the most successful. If, on the other hand, we seek greater equality of educational outcomes then we may need to treat individuals unequally from the outset, identifying the most disadvantaged and giving them enhanced (and so unequal) opportunities. For example, Younger and Warrington (2009) suggest that mentoring in school is most effective where targeted at pupils from families with the lowest expectations.

Indeed, in terms of learning and teacher-pupil relations, equality is a contentious concept, as arguably not all pupils can be treated 'in the same way'. Pupils with different learning needs will not thrive under a regime in which pupils are uniformly treated and expected to do the same work on an equal basis. Existing research with excluded pupils suggests that such 'equality' of treatment was perceived as highly unfair by pupils with other educational needs, and indeed, tended to exacerbate their disruptive or rebellious behaviour (Riley 2004). These complications explain some of the difficulty which pupils, and indeed adults, have in deciding whether they are treated unfairly or not.

Neither universalism nor relativism is able to explain our feelings of justice, for the criteria we apply are an adaptation of universal principles to the system of interactions in which we are placed (Boudon 1995). For example, a teacher may feel it is fair to over-reward a 'weak' pupil who submits good work, or a disruptive pupil on the day they behave well. Some well-behaved pupils may feel this is unfair while some others may accept it as an encouragement to pupils to be like them. Indeed, teachers may favour some pupils and penalise others, but they may also treat all pupils equally but unfairly. The latter occurs if they are aggressive or contemptuous towards *all* pupils or if injustice falls at random on one pupil or another. Furthermore, pupils may be sensitive not only to injustices towards themselves but also to those that affect others.

Few pupils feel themselves treated especially unfairly at age 15, an age at which they are no longer restrained from expressing this kind of feeling by a childish reverence towards their teachers (Grisay 1997), as shown in the difference in the attitudes of primary and secondary pupils (Dubet 1999). So, it seems that problems of unfairness are linked to the academic characteristics of the pupils as much as to their external characteristics. It may be that in some schools or classes the more serious transgressions (bullying, vandalism, violence, and disrespectful behaviour in general) of fairness which pupils experience come from other pupils and not from teachers. However, pupils may judge their teachers as being jointly responsible for these episodes since the teachers may appear incapable of managing discipline and social relationships.

The general sensitivity of a person to problems of justice or equity rather than to their own particular interests does vary. It is dependent on the system of values adopted by the individual, which in the case of a 14- or 15-year-old pupil is still likely to be strongly influenced (sometimes in oppositional form) by their family. The need to believe in a just world is not really felt by all people, at least not by all to the same extent (Gilles 2004). Therefore, some people may think that injustice could be, indeed must be, eliminated, while others may not. Evidently this belief influences individual perceptions of unfair behaviour. For example, our prior work (EGREES 2005) shows that the Italian respondents considered school to be a fair arena for meritocratic competition significantly less frequently than those from other countries. This normative judgment might be explained by the finding that the Italian respondents, compared to others, consider success in school to be a much less important factor for succeeding in life.

The attribution and anticipation of justice or injustice may vary according to the age and the characteristics of the individual (Kellerhals et al. 1988). These may also vary according to the characteristics of the group to which one belongs and to the situation in which they find themselves. Again, in our previous work (EGREES 2005) the judgments on justice in schools expressed by the least able pupils were often more severe than those expressed by others. It is impossible to know if this discrepancy arises because these 'less successful' pupils were more often the victims of school injustice or whether a defensive attitude induced them to emphasise external causal attributions.

The characteristics of the school may also matter, depending on the organisation of the national educational system, such as whether secondary level schooling is comprehensive or tracked. It might depend on institutional characteristics such as the prestige of the school, the headteacher's style of leadership and the structure of governance, or the nature and organisation of the school's pedagogic practice. And of course, it may also depend on the characteristics of those who attend the school and in particular, on the social and/or academic composition of the pupil population. Another influential context is the classroom, in particular its didactical practices and its social climate. Nevertheless, grasping the nature of this influence is not a trivial objective for our research. For example, a classroom that plans and claims to be fair, that encourages democratic discussion between teachers and pupils, may be supposed to be less affected by feelings of injustice. But also the opposite may occur. In fact, those claims and practices could have heightened the pupils' expectations of fair treatment and results, and consequently brought about an increasing feeling of injustice.

This leads us to think about the different criteria that young people might apply to explain or justify their experiences of (in)justice in different settings. As we have seen, principles of justice, such as equality of treatment, work only in limited contexts, from specific perspectives, and on some occasions. This makes any transparent judgement of fairness a confusing task. Yet, our own prior work with pupil perspectives has suggested that individuals show a high level of agreement about whether any situation or treatment is fair, and from this near-consensus we might begin to establish a better idea of what equity means for those participating in education.

Table 5.1 provides a summary of six possible principles of justice, orthogonal to four possible domains (or settings) in which pupils might wish to apply these principles. The point made here is that people quite properly and fairly apply different principles in different settings. For example, a pupil might agree that final outcomes such as public examination results could recognise merit and so differentiate between pupils (A in the table). However, the organisation of school procedures such as parent evenings should not be based on merit but should be open to all equally (B in the table). In education, some assets are, or should be, distributed evenly regardless of background differences – such as setting an equal teacher–pupil ratio for schools in different regions (C in the table), or equal respect shown to pupils by teachers (D). Other assets are, or might be, distributed in proportion between contribution and reward (E, F) – such as formal qualifications or punishments (Trannoy 1999). Further assets may be deliberately distributed unequally without consideration of contribution, such as greater attention given to disadvantaged pupils (G). Each column in Table 5.1 could also be further

Table 5.1   Some principles of justice and the areas in which they might be applied

| | Domains or settings | | | |
Principles	School procedures	Classroom interaction	Regular assessment	Final outcomes
Recognise merit	–	–	–	A
Equal opportunity	B	–	–	–
Equal outcome	C	–	–	–
Respect individual	–	D	–	–
Fair procedures	–	E	–	F
Appropriate treatment	G	–	–	–

Note: There could be more principles here, and there should be more settings, such as family and home, or wider society. But the table has been heavily simplified.

sub-divided, so that final outcomes might include minimum educational thresholds, such as basic literacy, which it would be fair for everyone to attain, and also graded examination results which it might be fair to allocate on merit.

All of these actions could be defended as equitable by the same person, apparently consistently, as they strive to remain fair while respecting differences between individuals or groups of pupils. Our research with pupils shows that individuals do hold these differing views at the same time, varying their use between discourse and practice, in different settings (EGREES 2005).

Some of the principles are themselves disputed concepts. For example, respect for the autonomy of the individual has been proposed as just (Jansen et al. 2006), but can be considered anti-educational if the purpose of education is to open minds to new ideas. To encourage autonomy in the sense of making people ignore expert advice might be considered ill-judged, for example, if it poses a risk to health, or safety (Hand 2006).

Views even vary according to pupils' recent experience. For example, when pupils are made to work on an individual basis in school they tend to favour the principle of recognising merit. But pupils asked to work co-operatively in classrooms tend to favour equality (Lerner 1980). Other researchers have also found that pupil reasoning about school rules varies across domains and categories such as relations, their protection, and etiquette (Thornberg 2008). Research with older students (in higher education) has also described distinct elements of their sense of fairness, such as those relating to respectful staff–pupil relations and to systemic fairness (Lizzio et al. 2007). In fact, pupils appear to distinguish between moral judgements of welfare and rights and justice (such as their effect on others), with transgressions which are wrong regardless of any laws, and social conventions (such as expectations and norms), with transgressions which are acceptable if no explicit rules prohibit them (Nucci 2001).

Each row in Table 5.1 could be further sub-divided, so that respect for the individual encompasses respect for personal autonomy, respect for differences between individuals, and the protection of a pupil's self-esteem. Equality of outcome could refer to the outcomes for all or, more narrowly, equality of outcomes for individuals of equivalent talent (Rawls 1971), or equality between socioeconomic groups. It could refer to equal achievement for equivalent work. Fairness of procedures could include equality before the 'law', either consistent or flexible interpretation of rules, or transparency, or the level of pupil participation in procedures.

Similarly, appropriateness of treatment could involve no discrimination or positive discrimination, unequal resources between advantaged and disadvantaged but equal resources for equal talent (Trannoy 1999), proportionate punishment for transgression, proportionate reward for performance, effort, or improvement, and proportionate final outcomes for performance, effort, or improvement. All of these could be considered 'fair', but many of them would be contradictory if applied together in the same domains or settings (Dubet 2006). What may seem fair on one principle may seem unfair on another, leading to constant critical rounds.

Of course, there will also be other important dimensions behind the table – such as the origin and victim of any injustice. The former might include authorities, schools, teachers, other pupils, and family members. The latter could be the individual, others such as peers or friends, a category of pupils, or all pupils. The precise combination of actors involved might affect our judgement about whether any principle should apply in a particular domain. We might be concerned about sub-groups of pupils, and wish to offer an advantage to those from a disadvantaged group from which the individual cannot 'escape'. Thus, geographic, institutional, and linguistic differences which are all changeable by the individual may be less important for some commentators than family background, sex, or innate disability which are likely to be permanent. However, there is also a view that no difference, in itself, is unjust and so an inequality is only unjust precisely insofar as it can be avoided by others (Whitehead 1991). Responsibility theory (Fleurbaey 1996, Roemer 1996) suggests a fair allocation of resources between individuals defined by their 'talent' – for which they are not responsible – and their 'effort' – for which they are. There is some evidence that pupils are sensitive to these differences. Pupils struggling because of inherent weakness or even a temporary problem like mobility or illness are excepted by other pupils from equal treatment. They are 'permitted' greater teacher concern because they are not to blame (Stevens 2009). They can be contrasted with those seen by other pupils as showing lack of willingness or interest, who are to blame and therefore must *not* receive extra attention. Struggling pupils only have a period of grace however. If they are not seen as making their best efforts to remedy the situation then they start to be blamed and so are responsible and therefore unworthy of help. Unfortunately, this argument falls down if effort or willingness is itself the product of motivation, which is itself a product of socioeconomic background for which individuals are not responsible.

How do we pick up on these issues via research that asks pupils for their views on a large-scale via a questionnaire for the most part, but does not constrain their responses, and can test the ideas in this book so far?

The pupil instrument

We focus here on the development of a questionnaire instrument, adapted for face-to-face and verbal completion where appropriate. Other data sources, our sample, and the context for the study are all described in the next chapter.

Our pupil-level questionnaire was developed in four parts, each part covering one or more of the principles of justice outlined so far, along with background and family items. The questionnaire was developed in two slightly differing versions for a field trial, in order to test the relevance of questions and themes raised, as well as the utility of different techniques for ordering and phrasing items. It was designed to last no more than 35 minutes. Pupils were asked about events occurring since the beginning of the current school year (Year 10 in England or Grade 9 elsewhere). The questionnaire, as a pilot, employed a mixture of scales including Likert scales, yes/no, categories, vignettes, and open-ended responses. It tried to measure pupils' perceptions of given events, such as unfair treatment by teachers, bullying by peers, and family relationships. The questionnaire was divided into four sections each examining a series of principles of justice as outlined in Table 5.1.

The *prevalence and character of injustice* section addressed the 'amount' and type of injustice pupils perceived that they experienced. Further, on the basis of existing research, (Smith and Gorard 2006), we were interested to see how pupils perceived the treatment of their peers. Earlier U.K. data had shown for example, that pupils generally thought they themselves were treated fairly, but that other pupils were treated unfairly to a much greater extent. This section deals with interactional justice at school (e.g., my teacher takes care not to humiliate me), distributive justice (e.g., my marks reflect the effort I make) and procedural justice (e.g., my teachers treat my opinions with respect even when we disagree). We were concerned also with the perpetrators of injustice, for example, primarily teachers, primarily other pupils, or both.

The *causes/sources of injustice section* was concerned with uncovering what pupils themselves feel are the causes of injustice. Questions and vignettes on hypothetical situations in school were included, giving us the possibility of comparing their actual experiences of fairness in school with their ideal model of a fair school. The items covered thus largely mirror questions asked about the pupils' lived experiences of injustice (e.g., teachers should take care not to humiliate pupils; my marks should reflect the effort I make). Pupils were also asked their opinions on whether ability or effort should be recognised, for example (A in Table 5.1), and whether respect for individual differences (D), appropriate treatment (G) or equality of opportunities (B) were more important for creating and defining a fairer school environment.

The next section addresses the so-called *'effects' of injustice* experienced at school. We were concerned to explore associations between perceived unfair treatment and academic, as well as social, confidence (e.g., school was a waste of time for me; I enjoyed working in groups with other pupils). Additionally, we wanted to examine how schooling experiences may be associated with wider attitudes and participation such as whether intense bullying on the basis of ethnicity might be associated with greater intolerance towards certain groups of people, or whether perceived exclusion and injustice on the part of teachers was associated with a reluctance to participate in community initiatives, or lowered aspirations.

It is likely that young people's sense of justice, their aspirations and expectations of their trajectories in society will be influenced by outside factors as well, such as parental background and their relationships with parents. The *external factors influencing sense of justice* section therefore included questions about the pupils' home background, asking about parental occupation and education, confidence with, and treatment by parents (e.g., my parents are usually interested in my well-being or any problems that I may have; my parents respect my opinion even when we disagree). Wider political and societal views were elicited through questions such as 'It is ok to lie to avoid being punished', 'People coming to live in Britain should be given equal rights' and 'I trust the British government to treat people fairly' [here phrased for the England sample]. The thinking was to map views on authority, equality of treatment, respect for individuals and appropriate behaviour outside school on pupils' views on in-school situations.

The ensuing and heavily piloted and re-designed instrument was then used in six countries, as described in Chapter 6.

6
Listening to Pupils in Different Countries

Introduction

Equity may be difficult to define. But, if our argument so far in this book is accepted, we may conclude that that it represents that sense of fairness which underlies our decisions about the key principles of justice, and how they may apply in different domains for a given set of actors. Equity is an important ideal for education, in terms of school as a lived experience as well as its longer-term outcomes for citizens and society. In specific situations there may be considerable agreement, among pupils, about what is fair and what is unfair. Indeed, pupils appear to have quite clear views on what is fair, and are often willing and able to express those views.

In setting out to answer the research questions that have emerged in the preceding chapters, from 'what schools are for' to 'what do pupils at school have to say about issues of equity', we conducted a large-scale study which looked at the experiences of fairness of an international group of young people. This chapter summarises our approach to that study, looking at the six countries involved, the schools and pupils who participated, and our various methods of data collection and analysis. The next section of the book then presents a summary of the evidence we uncovered and the conclusions we draw from it.

In this study we conducted fieldwork in Japan and five European countries, representing Northern, Southern, and Eastern Europe. A comparative approach was used, because it allowed us to consider the natural variation in school organisation as a potential explanation of any differences in the experience and sense of justice developed by pupils. This provides important indications for policy-makers and practitioners about the role of school organisation in creating equity and helping to form pupils' sense of justice. It was an international, large-scale test of the ideas in Chapters 3 and 4. The fieldwork took place in Belgium (French-speaking), the Czech Republic, England, France, Italy, and Japan.

Around 14,000 pupils in around 450 schools took part. In addition, we collated existing official data about the intake and performance of all participating schools, where available, such as that represented in the pupil level annual school census for England (PLASC, see Chapter 2). We created a brief supplementary school-level questionnaire unique to each country so that we had identical and comparable data on all schools. This instrument contained questions on the type of school, admissions policies, arrangement of classes according to ability, special educational needs, and voluntary schemes, and was sent to all participating schools for completion. All of these aspects were first piloted. We supplemented these with observations and field notes taken during administration of the survey. We use these various contextual sources as illustrations and potential explanations of the findings. We describe differences in outcomes and experiences between socioeconomic and ethnic groups, countries and school types. We have also modelled the plausible social and educational determinants of the different perceptions of justice among different types of pupils.

In each of the partner countries, a sample of up to 100 schools was selected from all mainstream secondary-age schools. Our focus on disadvantaged young people necessitated a concerted effort to reach also those pupils outside mainstream schooling, and to explore how their sense of justice in schools and in life may have been shaped by their less conventional school experiences. A diverse school (and pupil) mix was achieved. Within the mainstream school sample, we randomly selected one class of around 30 Year 10 pupils (Grade 9) in most cases, and more than one class in some cases (see below).

The initial results were presented to an international audience of teachers, school leaders and teacher trainers for discussion and feedback both on the presentation of results and on further analyses to be conducted. The comments and concerns of these practitioners have been integrated into our analysis as far as possible.

First here, we provide a brief reminder for international readers of some aspects of the school system of each country.

The research settings

Our fieldwork mostly took place in 2006/07, involving pupils with an average age of 14, in grade 9 of their secondary education. In all six countries, this means that such pupils are coming towards the end of their compulsory education, which Table 6.1 shows usually happens from ages 15 to 17. By that stage, pupils will have undertaken thousands of hours of formal education, based on around 1000 hours aged 12 to 14. They will have mostly been taught by females, except perhaps in Japan, which may influence their views on what is an appropriate future for men and women.

The majority of pupils are in publicly funded and maintained schools, except in Belgium where the majority are in private schools dependent on the government (Table 6.2). In addition, Italy, Japan, and the United Kingdom have a small but significant private independent sector. It will

Table 6.1 Aggregated characteristics of schooling in six countries, 2007

	Typical age range for schooling of 90%	Compulsory hours aged 12–14	Percentage female teachers, lower secondary
Belgium	3–17	960	60
Czech Republic	4–17	902	82
France	3–17	959	64
Italy	3–15	1016	75
Japan	4–17	869	40
United Kingdom	4–16	900	61

Source: Education at a glance (2007).

Table 6.2 Percentage of pupils in each type of school, by country, lower secondary, 2007

	Public	Government dependent	Private
Belgium	43	57	–
Czech Republic	98	2	–
France	79	21	–
Italy	96	–	4
Japan	94	–	6
United Kingdom	93	1	6

Note: Figures are percentages of all pupils in each type of provision, and should add up to 100 for each country.
Source: Education at a glance 2007.

be interesting to consider differences between the experiences of justice of pupils in these different kinds of schools.

There is more difference between these six countries in terms of the education of the wider population (Table 6.3). Adults in Japan and the United Kingdom have a generally higher level of education, according to these figures, and a slightly higher employment rate. In all other countries, a significant percentage of the population does not have even upper secondary levels of attainment, including almost half in Italy where the employment rate is also lowest. The situation in each of these countries may of course be different for pupils in schools today, but it will still be interesting to consider variation in terms of aspirations and expectations for the future.

Schools in Belgium (French-speaking)

In the French Community of Belgium, education is free of charge for a period of 12 years starting at the age of 6. Secondary education starts at the age of 12 with a common curriculum which lasts for 2 years (Eurydice 2006). Pupils are then tracked into general, technical or vocational routes, with different curricula attracting distinct social and academic populations (Demeuse et al. 2005, Demeuse et al. 2007). According to the curriculum followed, pupils will then get access either to higher education (after general or some technical curricula), or to post-compulsory education (vocational and some technical curricula). Vocational education can also lead directly to a 'vocational aptitude' certificate.

Table 6.3 Percentage of highest educational attainment by adults in six countries

	Upper secondary attainment	Tertiary attainment	Employment rate
Belgium	35	30	69
Czech Republic	77	13	73
France	43	25	71
Italy	38	13	63
Japan	60	40	75
United Kingdom	56	39	78

Note: Figures are percentages of adult population aged 25–64 in 2005, and will not add up to 100.

Source: Education at a glance 2007.

The Belgian education system is based on two principles of freedom of education, proclaimed in the Belgian Constitution. The first concerns the freedom given by law for pupils and parents to choose the school that suits them, initially in order to respect everyone's philosophical beliefs. The second relates to freedom of school management, leading to a system spread into 'réseaux', each having its own educational plan within which each school and teachers get their own pedagogical freedom. In practice, education is structured in three main 'réseaux' – public schools organised and financed by public authorities (the French Community), public grant-aided schools organised by the provinces or by municipalities, and private grant-aided schools (denominational, non-denominational, or pluralist) organised by private associations (non-profit, diocese, or congregation) or persons.

Numerous studies (such as Dupriez and Vandenberghe 2004, Dupriez and Dumay 2006, Vandenberghe 2000) have shown that the quasi-market of the Belgian education system results in important inequalities in school results because of the ensuing segregation of school intakes by socioeconomic background. The OECD PISA 2000 and 2003 studies revealed a strong attainment score discrepancy between the 25% of 15-year-old pupils with the highest socioeconomic background and the 25% of pupils with the lowest one. This may be due to high segregation between the intakes to different kinds of schools (see also Chapter 3).

Schools in the Czech Republic

Compulsory education in the Czech Republic lasts from the age of six or seven to age 15, – the end of lower secondary education. Pupils in this final grade can apply for further study to age 18 in three different streams – general (*gymnázia*), technical and vocational. The allocation of pupils to different streams is based on entrance examinations. Retention after the compulsory phase is very high (89%) and is based on a long-standing cultural tradition of education (Education at a Glance 2007). However the general stream is followed by only 20% of the age cohort compared to an EU-25 average of 37%. A majority of pupils thus complete their upper secondary education at technical and vocational schools (Eurydice 2007b).

For equity issues it is important to stress this selective nature of the Czech education system, which is based on early tracking and selection of pupils for more academically oriented programmes. The first stage of selection takes place at the age of 8 (3rd grade). Then pupils are able to apply for schools or classes with a specialist focus and which provide extended teaching in some subjects: foreign languages, physical education and sports, mathematics and natural sciences, music, visual arts, and information technologies. This specialised curriculum is followed from the 3rd year (languages) or 6th year (other subjects). Around 10% of basic school pupils attend these specialist schools. Parents show great interest in extended teaching in selected subjects – particularly languages (demand is twice as high as the number of places available) hoping for their children to achieve better results compared to other basic schools. Admission to this type of basic school is decided by school principals on the basis of entry examinations designed by the school and taken by children at the age of 8 (or 11). The second stage of selection is to the multi-year *gymnázia* (six- and eight-year-long programmes). While at basic schools the transition of 11-year-old pupils from the first to the second stage is automatic, admission to eight-year *gymnázia* programmes is based on written examinations designed by *gymnázia* teachers (normally in the mother tongue and mathematics), and, sometimes, intelligence or pupil aptitude tests. The intake numbers are determined by the school administration (approximately 10% of the relevant age group). The number of applicants for six- and eight-year *gymnázia* programmes is double the intake number.

The selective nature of the Czech educational system is even more pronounced if we take into account the degree of segregation of pupils with special educational needs into separate streams and special schools. The proportion of pupils with special needs educated separately in the Czech Republic is among the highest in the EU countries (5% according to Key Data on Education in Europe 2005).

Analysis of data from PISA and other international studies of pupil achievement such as TIMSS, IALS, and PIRLS (Straková 2003) suggests that the selective entrance examination to multi-year *gymnázia* at the age of 11 has resulted in pupils from the two lowest quintiles of SES making up only 15% of the pupil population at these selective schools. Thus, the existence of the multi-year *gymnázia* largely contributes to a reproduction of educational inequalities (Matějů and Straková 2005).

The Czech Republic operates a system of grade retention for pupils who do not make as much progress as their peers. Around 1% of pupils repeat a grade at primary level and another 1% at lower secondary level. Judgements about whether pupils are retained are based on teacher evaluations, since there is no system of statutory testing. In addition, around 5% of pupils drop out before the 9th grade.

According to PISA 2003, in the Czech Republic the impact of family background on pupil performance is very high and the difference in results between higher and lower SES schools is 1.5 times larger than the OECD average. School socioeconomic background explains 37% of the variance in the pupils' test results – the seventh highest value among the countries involved in PISA 2003. Ethnically, the Czech Republic remains a relatively homogenous society with a low proportion of immigrant children (less than 2%).

Schools in England

England, like the rest of the United Kingdom, has a universal, compulsory secondary school system for pupils from the age of 11, with around 650,000 pupils in any one cohort. Around 7% of the school population is in fee-paying schools. The remainder attend state-maintained schools usually catering for pupils aged 11–19, 13–19, or 11–16, with some other variations. A minority of secondary schools have a faith-base and are either voluntary-controlled or voluntary-aided. A further minority are deemed independent of local government authority control and these include Academies, City Technology Colleges and Foundation Schools. Around 150 maintained schools are selective, using an entry test at age 10 or 11. However, the vast majority of schools remain comprehensive in nature, although in principle the growing number of specialist curriculum schools are able to select up to 10% of their intake via aptitude (Harris and Gorard 2009).

All schools are required to complete a pupil level annual schools census (PLASC, see Chapter 2) which, combined with the NPD, provides hundreds of variables relating to each individual. For example, one of the variables records whether the pupil is from a family living in poverty. Around 15% of pupils in England live in poverty (officially defined). These are not evenly spread between schools. Most of the non-comprehensive, faith-based, or independent schools take fewer than expected poor children. Around one-third of the poor pupils would therefore have to exchange schools for them to be evenly spread across schools. This stratification by low income is greater in areas with diversity of schools, and has worsened in the last decade as schools have diversified (Gorard 2009c).

Using the 29 indicators from our prior work for the European Commission (EGREES 2005), we can say a little about justice in the U.K. schools system. Two conclusions about the United Kingdom leap out. Unusually, education is a near equitable process for both boys and girls (men and women), and for nationals, recent immigrants to the United Kingdom, and other nationals. The latter may be partly caused by, and the cause of, a very low gap in terms of income and other economic indicators between nationals and non-nationals. This equality is also reflected in equal cultural resources for nationals and non-nationals, and for males and females. And this pattern is then reflected in the near equal professional aspirations of boys and girls, and nationals and non-nationals. These patterns are very far from true of the EU as a whole. Educational support from teachers in the United Kingdom is near equal by gender, and by national origin of the pupils, and this is supported by the views of the pupils themselves. All of this means that school careers are similar in length and success rate by both sex and country of origin, and that by the end of formal schooling the qualification gap by sex and country of origin is relatively small. This, presumably, feeds back to the near equality in economic indicators.

None of the other patterns of equity for the United Kingdom are as clear as these two. In many respects, the 29 indicators portray U.K. society as both reasonably fair and relatively mobile (despite some recent erroneous claims to the contrary, such as in Gorard 2008e). The spread of family wealth is reasonable, and the welfare state principle means that there is a transfer of economic and cultural contribution from the most educated and high prestige occupations to the least educated and lowest prestige groups. For the countries where figures are available, the United Kingdom has by far the most socially mobile society, with surprisingly little impact of social origin on occupational status. Cultural resources are reasonably widespread by social class, and by educational attainment. There is little difference in the attention given by teachers to the education of different social classes, and this takes place in a largely comprehensive system of schooling, with lower than average segregation of pupils by test scores, family wealth, parental occupation, and country of origin. The effect of education itself on occupational prestige and social status is also low. Therefore, if valid, there is another virtuous cycle here of *relatively* little relationship, in comparison to several other EU countries, between class origin, ensuing educational attainment, and subsequent class destination. This is not the picture usually portrayed within the United Kingdom by policy-makers and the media (Gorard 2008e).

On the other hand, the length of initial education in the United Kingdom diverges substantially between social and economic groups. There is, for example, a considerable gap in the number of 'expected' years of education for the most and least educated 10%, and this may be partly why a low proportion of the population has attained the modal qualification by the age of 25–34. Teachers are, in the view of pupils, not giving sufficient or even equal support to poor readers at school. The impact of parental education on cultural practices and childrens' literacy is high, and the children of parents in the least prestigious occupations have markedly lower professional aspirations than their peers. All of these single indicator problems are worthy of further investigation.

Schools in France

Compulsory schooling in France starts at the age of six, and pupils normally spend five years in primary schools. A very high proportion of them will be made to repeat at least one grade of primary school – 18% of those starting school in 1997 had repeated a grade six years later (Repères et Références Statistiques, MEN, 2007).

After elementary school, pupils go to a comprehensive middle school (collège). This could be the public middle school of their catchment area (70%), or another public middle school (10%), or a private one (20%). Around 4% of middle school pupils belong to SEGPA (Sections d'Enseignement Général et Professionnel Adapté) or EREA (Etalissements Régionaux d'Enseignement Adapté). These are classes (SEGPA) or schools EREA) designed for pupils with severe learning difficulties. The SEGPA pupils (100,000 in the whole country) are included in the population of our new study, but the EREA pupils (10,000 in France) are not. At the end of the third grade of the middle school, some pupils may be oriented to more vocational tracks, and belong to 'troisièmes d'insertion' which are often embedded in vocational high schools. By the age of 14, about 80% of pupils go to the high school (lycée) while 20% (mostly the less able) are oriented towards a vocational school (lycée professionnel).

In France, égalité (or equality) has been a national motto since at least the national revolution at the end of the eighteenth century. In theory, this means that origin, religion, ethnicity, and family background are not meant to be a factor in the provision of public services. It was this that prompted a ban on conspicuous religious symbols in schools for pupils and teachers from 2005. This policy, and others like it, is certainly equal treatment but that does not, necessarily, make it fair (see Chapter 5).

Schools in Italy

In Italy the first cycle of compulsory education is split into two stages – primary education for children aged 6–11 and lower secondary for children aged 11–14. The second cycle consists of upper secondary education, for those aged 15–19, and a vocational training route which is followed upon completion of lower secondary school. In all, education is compulsory for 10 years – from six to 16 years of age (Eurydice 2008). Currently, upper secondary education is offered in *licei* which specialise in the classics, sciences, arts, or in sociopsycho-pedagogy. Vocational upper secondary education takes places in vocational, technical, or arts institutes. Schools in Italy have a relatively large degree of autonomy with regard to the teaching and administration of their programmes. For example, schools have considerable flexibility in determining the organisation of teaching time and curriculum content (Eurydice 2008).

In 2005, the graduation rate for upper secondary school pupils was 82%, which is equal to the OECD average for developed nations (OECD 2007a). Italy invested around 4.9% of GDP in education at all levels in 2004, this compares with around 5.9% for the United Kingdom and 5.4% for the EU-19 average (OECD 2007a).

Schools in Japan

The Japanese school system is modelled on a 6-3-3-4 structure. For the majority of pupils, that means six years of primary education (including kindergarten), three years of junior high school, three years of senior high school, and, for about 50% of pupils, four years of university (DeCocker 2002). Compulsory education ends with junior high school at the age of 15, although around 98% of pupils remain in education and proceed to senior high school. A high proportion of the population in Japan have completed upper secondary education, including nearly 90% of those aged 25 to 34. There are no national examinations *per se*. High stakes testing occurs at the end of junior high school, when pupils sit entrance examinations for senior high school, and again at the end of senior high school when pupils sit college or university entrance examinations. These entrance examinations are taken extremely seriously. Competition to secure a place in a highly regarded senior school is intense because they are seen as the gateways to an elite or high-quality university, which in turn can lead to high-status employment. The quality of senior high schools is traditionally estimated not by their examination results directly, but by the number of pupils they place in the top tier of Japan's universities and at elite universities, such as the Universities of Tokyo or Kyoto in particular (Roesgaard 1998). According to Lynn (1988), the achievements of these leading schools receive wide media coverage in Japan and are of great interest to the population in general who follow their progress avidly 'somewhat as they do of sports teams in the West' (p. 28). One aspect of the Japanese school system that has received much attention from overseas is the *juku* or 'cram school'. Many Japanese pupils begin to attend the *juku* during junior high school. These are often commercially run enterprises, although they might equally consist of small groups run in the home by pupils' mothers, who provide coaching lessons for high school entrance examinations. It is estimated that at any one time 6.5 million of Japan's 15 million school children attend *juku* or equivalent (Manzo 2002). Pupils would normally attend *juku* after school, often for up to two hours, twice per week.

The annual compulsory instruction time for a seven to eight year-old varies between 981 hours in Australia and 530 in Finland, with the OECD average level being 758 hours. The corresponding Japanese time is, at 712 hours, below the average. The situation is similar at the secondary level of education. However, Japan's position on schooling outcomes is not only strong in quantitative terms, but the OECD PISA assessment of the knowledge and skills of 15-year-olds in key subject areas shows Japan to be one of the best-performing countries in terms of both the quality and equity of schooling outcomes. For example, 89% of Japanese males (OECD average 82%) and 60% of females (OECD average 65%) with an upper secondary qualification are in employment. For those without an upper secondary qualification, the figures are 79% of males (OECD average 72%) in employment, and 53% of females (OECD average 49%).

Despite above-average spending per primary-level pupil, Japan has, with 28.6 pupils per class, one of the largest average class sizes at the primary level of education, second only to Korea, and in all but nine countries there are between 16 and 21 pupils per primary-level class (the OECD average is 21.4). Similarly, in lower secondary education there are on average 33.8 pupils per class in Japan, far above the OECD average of 24.1. Of the 21 countries for which comparable data are available, only Korea has an even higher average class size at the lower secondary level. This is partly due to higher teacher salaries, especially for the unusually high proportion of male teachers.

In Japan, the percentage of females obtaining tertiary-type A education are below the OECD average for all fields of study. Only 31% of graduates in life sciences, physical sciences, and agriculture are females in Japan, whereas the OECD average level is 51%. For all fields of education combined, the OECD average percentage of female graduates of tertiary-type A programmes is 54%, while in Japan the same level is only 40%, the lowest of all 27 countries with comparable data.

The national samples

Our main study was conducted between April and July 2007 in the European countries, and comprised a target sample of 100 schools in each country. We wanted at least one class of around 25–30 pupils per school. We chose to focus on Grade 9 pupils (14- to 15-year-olds) as this was considered to be towards the lower limit at which young people begin to form sustained views on social and political matters and more abstract concepts, such as equity, social responsibility and citizenship. The pupils were around 14 years old, but the practices of fast-tracking or retention in some countries increased this age range. It was administratively simpler to deal with teaching units as far as possible, and likely to lead to greater co-operation from schools, and fuller response rates from pupils.

Each partner provided a list of all schools and educational institutions in their country with Grade 9 pupils (or 14-year-olds where no grade is specified). Each school had an identifier and an estimate of the number of pupils on roll in Grade 9 (either the full-time equivalent of the number on roll in Grade 9, or an estimate of this derived from the total number on roll). The list was sorted into size order, and divided into notional sub-lists using the required sampling fraction (n/100), and cases then selected randomly from within these sub-lists of approximately equal-sized schools. Each country selected 200 schools. The first 100 of these was approached. The next 100 provided back up schools in case of refusal.

Once a school (or institution) was selected, its address was added to its existing record and the school approached via initial letter to the head teacher, followed by email and telephone calls to the head teacher, or head of year/subject head, backed up by a project outline and sample questions.

Between 70 and 85 schools were obtained in each partner country, giving an approximate total of 450 schools (with around 14,000 pupils) for the study, plus the special cases (see below and Chapter 9). Once they had agreed, questionnaire packs were sent to participating schools, including a short manual for the administrating teacher and a self-addressed, stamped envelope for returning completed forms in. Returned questionnaires were then sent to the research team for scanning (using optimal mark recognition) and data cleaning before analysis.

Our focus on disadvantaged or marginalised youth necessitated a concerted effort to reach also those pupils outside mainstream schooling, and to explore how their sense of justice in schools and in life may have been shaped by their less conventional school experiences. Six 'case-study' institutions in each country were selected in addition to the main sample, to include PRUs, juvenile detention centres, and special schools likely to hold a high proportion of the most disadvantaged pupils. Interviews with pupils in these schools (approximately 10 pupils per school) took place in September 2007. These pupils responded in several ways. Some were able to complete the questionnaire, some were given an abbreviated version to complete, some had questions read and their answers written for them, and some took part as though it were a structured interview.

A brief set of school-level questions unique to each country was designed so that we had identical and comparable data on all schools (like that represented in the PLASC for England, see above and Chapter 2). This also allows us to compare pupils' notions of justice and their experiences of schools across a range of educational settings and in different pupil mixes. Questions included the geography of the school, any programmes it was associated with, how its places were allocated, and whether pupils are taught in mixed ability groups or not. This form was either completed by the class teacher while the pupils completed their survey, or was completed by a school leader subsequently.

The pilot study

We conducted a field trial of two slightly different versions of the pupil questionnaire, based on our conceptual background (as discussed in Chapter 5), in October to November 2006, in five partner countries – France, Belgium (French-speaking), Italy, the Czech Republic, and England. The two questionnaires were largely identical, but had a range of different and differently worded questions allowing us to trial and compare these. In each country, we piloted the proposed sampling process for 10 schools and one case study of pupils being educated outside mainstream schooling, with two Grade 9 teaching groups in each school being asked to participate for the duration of a regular registration or Citizenship/PSHE type class.

Approximately 350 pupils took part in the pilot for each country, giving a total of 1,820 pupils from 92 classes. We piloted the sampling, access arrangements, both pupil and school-level questionnaires and an administrator's manual, technical documents, translation of all pilot instruments into French, Italian, and Czech, preparation of the pilot sample, procedures for contacting schools, duplication of questionnaires, and preliminary analysis of results. A school-level questionnaire was given to the head teacher at each school to complete and return to the national research teams by post. It was agreed that members of each research team would be present in schools when the classroom-level questionnaire was administered to pupils, in order to record pupil comments and other issues relevant to revision/improvement of the instrument, as well as to monitor the process.

Methodologically, this trial proved very useful in terms of improving access to disadvantaged pupils, as well as revising the pupil instrument. In general, the instrument worked well, had a high completion rate, and we found that the different ways of asking the same questions were unrelated to the achieved responses. The pilot study brought a range of new issues to our attention, particularly related to the content of the questionnaires, but also national differences in securing access to schools, ineffective translation of items and so on. Among other things, it was decided that a school-level questionnaire would be ineffective in most countries and a classroom-level questionnaire for teachers (in addition to the one for pupils) was developed instead.

The achieved sample

On average, the achieved sample of schools in each country was just over 80% of the ideal of 100. However, the number of replacement schools that had to be used was so high, and the differences in the number of classes per school (see below) mean that we do not treat them from here onwards as a genuine cluster-randomised sample. We are more concerned with the effect sizes of differences between groups of pupils and schools than with the probability of being able to generalise from each national sample to the population of that country. Replacement also meant that there are a larger number of cases in some countries than others (Table 6.4). The primary unit of sampling is the school in each country, and for any analysis at the school level having more than one class per school creates a better estimate of the school-level picture. For any level of analysis at the class level, the number of classes per school is largely irrelevant. However, any analysis at the country level needs to take the differences in number of classes per school into account. Schools with more responses for reasons other than size of school/class may bias the national picture. For example, one of the schools with multiple classes in England was a private fee-paying school for girls. Therefore, any analysis using all cases will over-represent girls at private school. In all countries, from 48% to 52% of pupils were male (and of course female), while the overall sample was 50% male and 50% female.

Table 6.4 Number of pupil forms returned, by country

	Forms	Percentage of total
Belgium (Fr)	1608	12
Czech Republic	1512	11
England	2836	21
France	3627	26
Italy	2992	22
Japan	1191	9

Characteristics of the young people who participated in the study

The pupil questionnaire gathered a large amount of background information on the young people who participated in the study. This enabled us to examine the relationship between this contextual data and young people's views and experiences of fair treatment (Chapter 8). This is of particular interest when we consider the views of young people who appear to be the most marginalised in school. In this section, we summarise the characteristics of our sample, according to their country of birth, home language, academic attainment, sex, and aspirations. We also describe the social, educational, and occupational characteristics of their families.

Pupil background characteristics

The majority of the young people who participated in our study told us that they were born in the country in which they were now being educated (Table 6.5). In this, and many of the subsequent tables, readers will notice that we do not present data for the Japanese sample. The reason for this is that questions which relate to the pupils' background and other family characteristics were considered by our Japanese partners to be too sensitive to be included in our survey. Therefore our analysis of the findings which relate to the different groups of pupils within each country, tend to omit those from Japan. The Czech Republic, as reported here, appears to have a particularly static population.

The majority of all pupils, regardless of where they live, told us that the language of the survey was the same as the language they spoke at home (Table 6.6). France had the highest proportion of young people who reported that they did not speak French at home. As above,

Table 6.5   Percentage of pupils born
in country of survey

Belgium	89
Czech Republic	97
France	94
Italy	93
England	94
Total	93

Table 6.6   Percentage of pupils speaking
language of survey at home

Belgium	79
Czech Republic	93
France	71
Italy	83
England	84
Total	81

Table 6.7   Percentage of pupils reporting high, average or low
marks at school

	High marks	Average marks	Low marks
Belgium	29	62	9
Czech Republic	26	68	6
France	24	59	18
Italy	11	73	16
England	41	53	6
Total	25	59	12

the Czech Republic appeared to have the most settled and uniform
population.

In the absence of a single internationally comparable measure of
academic attainment, we asked pupils to tell us whether, in their opinion, they had tended to receive mainly high, average or low marks
in school for that year (Table 6.7). While it is difficult for us to verify the accuracy of their estimations, these responses do give us some
indication of the level at which the young people perceive themselves

to be achieving in school. We are then able to draw some tentative comparisons between these self-reports and their experiences of fair treatment in school (see Chapters 7 and 8). Similar proportions of pupils from Belgium, the Czech Republic, and France report that they achieve high marks. A relatively small proportion of Italians report high marks, while a very different and more positive pattern appears for English pupils.

In England, the National Curriculum requires testing in English, Mathematics and Science for all 14-year-olds (Year 9) in state-maintained schools. These are high stakes tests, reported as levels in the range 3 to 7, affecting league tables at school level and setting and examination tier entry for pupils (see also Chapter 7). So pupils tend to be aware of what levels they reach. Asking the English respondents to report their Year 9 Levels has allowed us to gain some indication, albeit still self-reported, of the actual academic achievement of the English sample. In England, national standards are such that young people aged 14 are expected to achieve at least National Curriculum Level 5. In 2007, 74% of 14-year-olds achieved Level 5 or above in English, 76% in Mathematics, and 73% in Science. The vast majority of pupils in our sample were achieving at or above the expected levels in national tests at age 14 (Table 6.8). Indeed, almost half of the pupils who provided a response to these questions were working at the highest levels of 6 or above.

Our cross-tabulation of the data in Table 6.7 (self-reported attainment) with that in Table 6.8 (more objective attainment) suggests that the English sub-sample is reporting similar standards in response to the two questions. Perhaps therefore we can assume that pupils in other countries, for whom we do not have the more objective measure, are also reasonably accurate in their assessments.

Table 6.8 Attainment at National tests for 14-year-olds, England only

	English	Mathematics	Science
Level 3	2	2	2
Level 4	9	8	9
Level 5	26	17	23
Level 6	31	24	28
Level 7	15	31	20
Non-response	17	17	18

Table 6.9   Percentage of pupils wanting a professional or intermediate occupation

Belgium	87
Czech Republic	74
France	78
Italy	76
England	83
Total	79

Pupils were asked to provide an indication of the type of job they wanted in the future. Occupations were grouped according to whether or not they represented traditionally 'professional' (e.g., doctor, scientist, lawyer), 'intermediate' (e.g., police officer, office clerk, motor mechanic), or 'working' class (e.g., postal or factory worker, labourer) occupations. Respondents were asked to choose the group which most closely resembled the job that interested them. They were also given the option of selecting a 'don't know' or a 'I don't really want a job at all' category. We focus here on the percentage wanting a professional or intermediate occupation (Table 6.9). However, we make no judgement of the desirability or appropriateness of each pupil's aspirations. For one thing, the pupil may simply be making a rational choice of career based on their current interests and academic attainment. Most pupils in all countries wanted a professional/intermediate job later, with the lowest proportion in the Czech Republic.

The characteristics of the young people's families

We now describe the sample involved in this study in terms of the characteristics of their parents. As expected, most parents are reported to have been born in the country in which the survey took place (Table 6.10). The figures are generally similar for both mothers and fathers. Again the population of the Czech Republic is the most clearly indigenous. At 36% the figure for mothers born in England is very low. This may reflect the respondents' confusion over whether the question was specific to England or to the other countries of the United Kingdom, although the same level of confusion does not appear for fathers. Either way, the figure for the English sample is anomalous, and assumed to be incorrect (i.e., that it is the result of an electronic coding and reading error that can no longer be corrected).

Table 6.10   Percentage of parents born in
the country of survey

	Mother	Father
Belgium	70	68
Czech Republic	93	94
France	77	74
Italy	89	91
England	36	81
Total	72	81

Table 6.11   Percentage of parents reported
to have attended university

	Mother	Father
Belgium	31	31
Czech Republic	21	22
France	21	22
Italy	24	24
England	27	28
Total	24	25

Although it is a widely used measure of family SES, young people's reports of their parents' educational histories have the potential to be unreliable (Gorard 1997). In this study we asked young people to tell us whether or not their mother and father had attended university (Table 6.11). While there are arguably some difficulties with such a relatively crude measure of parental educational level, this does provide an indication of which pupils came from families who are, or had been, engaged in education beyond the compulsory phase. The figures for participation in university level education were similar for both fathers and mothers – between 20 and 30% – and were broadly similar across countries.

As with the question on occupational aspirations described earlier, respondents were asked to select the occupation which most closely resembled those of their parents (Table 6.12). Across all countries 13% of mothers were identified as having no job. England had the largest

Table 6.12 Percentage of parents with professional/
intermediate occupational status

	Mother	Father
Belgium	56	62
Czech Republic	56	49
France	52	52
Italy	47	58
England	67	75
Total	55	59

proportion of fathers who were employed in professional or intermediate level jobs, with the Czech Republic having the lowest. This may reflect the nature of the achieved sample (see above) as much as any difference in national employment patterns.

Summary

This chapter has summarised the approach that we used in collecting the data for our international study into young people's experiences of fairness in school as well as in wider society. We have illustrated some of the main characteristics of the national education systems of the schools that we surveyed, explained the stages in the piloting and sampling process, and described some of the background characteristics of our sample and of their families. Using the datasets we have generated, the next four chapters present a summary of some of the key results.

Part IV

Illustrating Pupils' Sense of Justice

7
International Comparisons of Pupil Experiences of Justice

Introduction

We described some of the characteristics of our large sample of international pupils – 14,000 young people from six countries – in Chapter 6. Here we summarise their views on justice both at school and in the wider world, and some of the experiences that might have helped shape those views, on a country by country basis. The ideas and motivations behind some of the responses presented here are complex to unravel, as they may be linked to the cultures and expectations of the different countries in which the young people live. Therefore, one aim of this chapter is to summarise the main themes which emerge and to consider the extent to which young people's experiences of equity are similar, and also different, in each of the national contexts which we explore. Ensuing chapters look at the experiences of different groups across all countries, and also put this all together in a multivariate analysis. In all of these chapters we present the questionnaire results, usually in tables, supplemented with a selection of open-ended and face-to-face comments provided by young people (and recorded in England and Japan).

Of course, any difference in the views of pupils across countries may be due to a host of factors. It could be a result of random and/or systematic sampling variation, or a subtle change in the meaning of the questions when translated into different languages. So the manifest differences we highlight here, and in the next four chapters, as potential outcomes of differences in the structure and experience of schooling at national level, are selected to be large or repeated, and consistent with other data, such as the comments of pupils and the information about each country context (see Chapter 6). For the present, we focus on differences and similarities between countries.

The treatment of individual pupils by teachers

The picture of pupil teacher relationships from our survey is a generally positive one, with 60% to 70% of pupils reporting that they get along well with teachers, and only 10% disagreeing with this (Table 7.1). In summary, less than 10% of pupils in all countries reported that school had been a waste of time for them. The other noticeable finding, when looking at the results on a country by country basis, is how similar many of them they are. The questions with high agreement are the same across all countries, as are the questions with low agreement.

One feature of the responses from the Japanese pupils was the relatively high number of neutral answers – neither agree nor disagree. For example, almost half of the pupils from Japan offered a neutral response

Table 7.1   Percentage of pupils agreeing with each statement about their relationship with teachers

	Belgium (Fr)	Czech Republic	England	France	Italy	Japan
I got along well with my teachers	70	72	63	66	59	65
Teachers treated me no better or worse than other pupils	62	59	42	62	58	52
Teachers encouraged me to make my own mind up	50	48	56	51	66	34
Teachers treated my opinion with respect even if we disagreed	48	29	42	45	49	29
I was always treated fairly by my teachers	47	35	39	46	51	47
I trusted my teachers to be fair	40	48	59	35	42	35
Teachers have been interested in my well-being	35	42	42	34	44	35
Teachers got angry with me in front of the whole class	33	48	44	36	25	34
I felt as though I was invisible to most teachers	28	12	17	33	23	14

Note: This table shows only a selection of the indicators. All others show the main patterns described in the text.

to the statement 'Teachers treat my opinions with respect'. A similar proportion were neither able to agree nor disagree with statements about whether or not their teachers encouraged them to make up their own minds (irony noted). This level of neutral response was higher than that from the other countries involved in the study. This means that for both agree and disagree the percentages from Japan tend to be lower for most questions. One possible explanation is that the concepts may translate poorly into Japanese, and so the key meanings behind these questions were unclear to the Japanese participants – although nothing in their fuller comments suggests this. A better explanation is that the issues we were asking about were less familiar to this group of pupils. Perhaps they have not considered that there might be an egalitarian relationship between teacher and pupil, and so such questions led to a genuinely neutral response on this occasion.

Pupils from Japan seem, with the caveat noted, to report less autonomy in their learning – being less positive about being allowed to make their own mind up, and having their opinions treated with respect. One says:

> [Teacher] listens to the opinions of pupils who have good marks, but he ignores others who have low marks or who he does not like. This is strange. Teachers should not differentiate pupils. (Japan, male)

Of course, this kind of experience is not limited to Japan:

> I expressed an opinion in class, my teacher disregarded it, then another pupil said the same thing and she congratulated them. My opinion was not respected. (England, female)

> When a teacher doesn't explain a 'subjunctive' because they think it will confuse you but the rest of the class seem to understand but I didn't and they refused to explain it to you. (England, female)

Looking at these indicators of teacher behaviour as a group, there is a tendency for pupils from the Czech Republic to be less positive about their teachers' explanation of topics, the respect they give to pupil opinions, and their general fair treatment. Nearly half of Czech pupils reported that a teacher had been angry with them in front of the class that year. Overall, the reported picture in Italy is more positive, as it is in Belgium and France except that a substantial minority of pupils in both countries report feeling invisible to their teachers. The situation in England is somewhat mixed. Of interest for future discussion is the observation that teachers in England appear to be more discriminatory (only 42% treated the respondent pupil no better or worse than others), and more likely to get angry with individuals, but also more trusted to be fair to pupils. This could be an indication of a Rawlsian principle discussed in Chapter 5 that it is fair to treat people differently when that difference can be justified. In some circumstances, not to differentiate is more unfair.

However, we should also consider that less than half of pupils consider their teachers this year to be fair, interested in pupils' well-being, and so on. Whether pupil views are accurate or not, the fact that they report this is should be a concern across all countries. As we shall see below, there is a possible tension between the nature of the fair treatment that pupils report that they ought to experience and the level of attention that teachers might feel is commensurate with effective pedagogic practice.

A very similar picture to above appears in Table 7.2, such as less agreement overall from pupils in Japan, but otherwise considerable similarity across countries and groups. Intriguingly, the responses in each country are almost exactly the same to the question about marks reflecting quality of work and effort. Perhaps pupils do not distinguish the two, or perhaps they generally believe that effort leads to quality. There is more variation in the item about whether teachers continued explaining until the pupil understood. This may be partly to do with tracking and setting. Presumably, in heavily tracked or segregated systems, the range of pupil ability or talent in any classroom will be lower than in genuinely comprehensive settings. This might make it easier for teachers

Table 7.2   Percentage of pupils agreeing with each statement about distributive justice

	Belgium (Fr)	Czech Republic	England	France	Italy	Japan
My marks usually reflected the quality of my work	62	70	64	59	58	49
Teachers continued explaining until I understood the topic	60	41	48	52	69	47
My marks usually reflected the effort I made	59	69	63	56	56	48

to carry all pupils along with their explanations. But while this might account for a higher score in Belgium, it does not really explain why the figure is so low in the Czech Republic nor so high in Italy. This issue is considered again in Chapter 8 in light of responses by different groups of pupils.

The treatment of all pupils by teachers

In fact, pupils are somewhat less content with their teachers' relationships with pupils more generally than they are with their own relationship with teachers (Table 7.3). Sometimes this is, presumably, simply a matter of frequency. For example, more pupils report having seen a teacher get angry in front of pupils than report a teacher being angry with them in front of pupils. This is only to be expected, if the reports are accurate and not all pupils have been subject to this treatment. In other respects the treatment experienced by each individual and all pupils is remarkably similar. For example, around 40% of pupils said that teachers treated their opinions with respect (Table 7.1) and around 40% also said that teachers treated all pupils' opinions with respect

Table 7.3 Percentage of pupils agreeing with each statement about the relationship of most pupils with teachers

	Belgium (Fr)	Czech Republic	England	France	Italy	Japan
Teachers got angry with a pupil in front of the whole class	77	88	60	80	70	67
Teachers gave extra help to those pupils who needed it	67	55	66	62	68	30
Hard-working pupils were usually treated the best	62	68	67	69	59	41
Teachers had favourite pupils	60	76	69	64	58	63
Teachers respected pupils' opinions even if they disagreed with them	49	31	39	46	46	22
All pupils were treated the same way in class	31	34	30	31	38	34

(Table 7.3). This could, of course, be lack of sensitivity to the difference in the questions on the part of respondents, but we have no evidence that this is so and on other questions, such as about teachers getting angry, the responses for self and others are very different. We assume, therefore, that these are useful responses, and that this represents a real gap between what pupils want and what they receive from teachers (see below).

Again the levels of agreement from Japan tend to be lower (see above), and again there is broad agreement across all countries. Around one-third of pupils in all countries report that all pupils were treated the same in class (not necessarily the fair approach), but around two-thirds reported that teachers had favourites – almost certainly not deemed a fair approach. In fact, the issue of favourites led to many strongly worded complaints such as:

> I try really hard in all my tests and homework, but I don't get grades which reflect the effort I put into it. Also some teachers have their favourites and ignore others. (England, female)

> When teachers go to their favourite pupils and then never get time to see you then ask for you to stay after school to get help, when you have after school activities – happened to me its unfair. (England, female)

> Teachers treat their favourite pupils in different way from other pupils. I always think it is unfair. When their attitude towards me is very cold, or they ignore me, I feel irritated. (Japan, male)

> It is strange that some teachers favour pupils. Although a pupil makes an effort, teachers do not lead such a pupil to improve if they do not like him. It is strange that there are big differences in teachers' attitudes. (Japan, female)

> In English lessons, when a pupil cannot translate a sentence, the teacher always calls the specific pupil and says 'X, translate it'. It has been like this since I was in the first year. I do not get angry about it anymore, but I'm disgusted with it. I am disappointed with this school because there is a teacher who shows they have favourites. (Japan, female)

Although the questionnaire responses about favouritism from England are in line with those of other countries, and just under 70% of English pupils thought that hard working pupils were treated the best, the comments from the Japanese and English pupils do point to a slightly different perspective on which groups of pupils are treated more fairly by their teachers. The English pupils tend to be concerned that their peers who were less academically successful or who misbehaved in class claimed the lion's share of the teacher's attention and praise. Among the Japanese pupils it was overwhelmingly the pupils who achieved the highest marks who were seen to be favoured. Put simply by one Japanese pupil: 'Teachers are kind to those who have good marks'.

The situation as described for pupils more generally is, as expected, more negative than reported for each individual (Table 7.4). Only around half of all pupils believe that marks are given because they are 'deserved', fewer report that pupils are punished fairly, and even fewer think that their teachers explain things in such a way as to allow all pupils to understand. These are serious charges that appear in every country and for every group of pupils. They are no longer thinking about themselves here (a fact reflected in the different levels of agreement to these items compared to Table 7.2, for example), and so this is not an attempt at self-justification or over-sensitivity to their own position. Something is not right.

Pupils report that being treated differently is not necessarily problematic if this differential treatment is deemed appropriate and fair. The open responses show, however, that this is not always happening. Teachers do not appear to be sensitive to the more subtle distinctions drawn by pupils. Put another way, teachers appear to be mis-applying

Table 7.4   Percentage of pupils agreeing with each statement about distributive justice for most pupils

	Belgium (Fr)	Czech Republic	England	France	Italy	Japan
Some pupils were punished more than others for the same offence	61	53	70	64	48	49
Pupils usually got the marks they deserved	58	60	51	54	46	48
Teachers punished bad behaviour fairly	46	45	37	42	47	40
Teachers continued explaining until all pupils understood the topic	40	37	43	34	47	29

a criterion of justice to the wrong domain. One recurring example of apparent inequity stems from respondents' observations that teachers were inconsistent and unfair when punishing pupils, and that teachers had favourites and that certain groups of pupils (for example, hard working pupils) were treated better than others. The issue of even-handed punishment is the one which generated the most complaints from pupils. The majority also believed that teachers did not punish evenly and fairly for the same 'offence'. Interestingly, however, all of the given examples are about the pupil themselves rather than others:

> At this one incident I got a detention for looking at the clock by Ms T. I think that is unfair because it was a harsh punishment and in most peoples' opinion I did nothing wrong. (England, male)

> My chemistry teacher sent me out of the classroom for the whole lesson for sitting in the wrong seat. (England, sex unknown)

> My teacher sent me out of the classroom (not school policy) for sneezing in class. The same teacher earlier on in the year sent me out again for no apparent reason. Both times he claimed I was attention seeking. (England, male)

> When a pupil can wear their own coat throughout the class and another pupil wears a ring and is asked to remove it. Certain pupils are allowed to sleep in lessons. (England, female)

> In our school we recently had a new PE teacher. I forgot my PE kit and so did another girl in our class. She fined me £2.50 and not the other girls saying that it was her first time for forgetting the PE kit. (England, female)

> When I made the same mistake as another pupil, the teacher shouted at me and struck me, but he did not get angry with another pupil and he just laughed at him. (Japan, male)

> When my friend and I did something wrong at school, I was scolded for a long time, but my friend was scolded a little. Both of us should have been scolded equally because we did the same thing. (Japan, male)

> In the history class, I left my book and I got yelled at for five or ten minutes and the teacher hit my head about ten times, also, I was called back after the class. When another pupil, who was cleverer than I, left his book, he was told only to go home to bring it, but he was neither hit nor called back afterwards. (Japan, male)

Some pupils dye their hair and behave aggressively, and teachers cannot deal with them and they are not disciplined. But teachers are very strict to some other people who did something wrong. Teachers are scared of some pupils and it affects our lessons. (Japan, female)

When I brought my mobile phone to school, I got yelled at very severely so that I did not want to come to school. But when another pupil, who is always defiant and behaves violently, brought one in, the teacher did not say anything to him. When I coloured my hair, I also got yelled at, but the teachers did not say anything to that pupil when he coloured his hair. (Japan, male)

It is these episodes, as much as anything, that help pupils decide that a school or a teacher is unfair. Discrimination in terms of need, effort and attainment are all accepted or even preferred, but to be punished more harshly than another for the same thing leads to lingering resentment. It is not punishment or reward in itself that is objected to. These things are not, for pupils, like respect that all or none should have. But they must be warranted and distributed proportionately and clearly.

The interaction of pupils with other pupils

As in their interaction with teachers, pupil reports of their relationships with other pupils are mostly positive and largely similar across all six countries. Over 90% of pupils have good friends, less than 10% are left out by others, and only around 7% feel invisible to their peers (Table 7.5). Most pupils report enjoying working with others, and having a friend who gets low marks at school. It is important to stress these positive results and similarities so that discussion of any differences is considered in a proportionate way.

The overall figures for negative episodes involving other pupils are, thankfully, low in all countries. But they are still substantial because of what they (could) represent. School can be a frightening and disagreeable experience. Again, Italy and to a slightly lesser extent Belgium and France have the most positive (or least negative) reports. Bullying, violence and so on are relatively low in Italy. The proportion of pupils from the Czech Republic and Japan with a friend from another country is very low, presumably partly explained by recent immigration patterns in those countries. Nevertheless, there could be issues of integration there that need addressing. Unsurprisingly perhaps, pupils whose family come from outside the test country are more likely to have friends in the same position (see Chapter 8). An alarmingly high proportion of pupils

Table 7.5 Percentage of pupils agreeing with each statement about their relationship with other pupils

	Belgium (Fr)	Czech Republic	England	France	Italy	Japan
I have good friends in school	94	89	92	94	89	88
I had a friend(s) who gets low marks at school	81	76	72	84	81	72
I had a friend(s) who doesn't come from country of test	80	28	50	65	58	29
I enjoyed working with other pupils	79	77	80	78	57	61
Something of mine was stolen	21	31	31	20	14	19
I was left out by other pupils	13	8	12	14	6	10
I was deliberately hurt by another pupil(s)	10	9	22	10	4	26
I was bullied by other pupils	8	4	15	9	5	11
I felt as though I was invisible to my school mates	7	8	7	8	6	10

in the Czech Republic and England (31%) report having had something stolen by another pupil at school in that year. Pupils are notorious for attributing lost articles as theft, but the differences between countries here are worthy of more attention in future chapters.

The number of pupils deliberately hurt by others in quite high in England and Japan, and bullying is also more widely reported in England. Bullying is more widespread among the lower achievers. However, it is not clear whether this is an indictment of the English system, evidence of the unconscious victim thesis in other countries, or enhanced awareness of bullying among English children. It can be that programmes intended to reduce negative experiences such as bullying lead, ironically, to an increase in reports. However, the number of pupils reporting being hurt by another pupil is also high in England. This suggests that the higher rate of bullying reported there is not to do with the phenomenon of unconscious victims in other countries or awareness in England. Interestingly the experiences of the Japanese pupils with regard to bullying itself were little different from those reported by the other pupils involved this study. This pattern is in contrast to other recent research which has suggested that Japanese pupils experience high levels of bullying both from other pupils and from their teachers. Perhaps there was confusion or conflation here in the various translations between being hurt and being bullied.

Bullying by pupils is intrinsically unfair and unpleasant, but for several pupils the teachers also bear some responsibility for not dealing with it adequately, or in some examples equitably:

> When I said to a teacher that I was bullied, he did not listen to me. But when his favourite pupil went to say that he was bullied, the teacher listened to him. (Japan, male)

Views on justice in schools

In assessing what it is that pupils report a school or teacher should be like, we begin to identify the criteria of justice they are using. There is near unanimity across all countries that all pupils should be respected (Table 7.6). At least within the domains or settings represented by school (see Chapter 5), respect for all pupils by teachers is a universal, even where there is disagreement between teacher and pupil. But there is also widespread agreement that in other domains all pupils do not need to be treated equally. It is, according to these respondents, fair for pupils struggling through no fault of their own to be given extra attention (presumably as a temporary measure, see below). It is also fair for teachers to allocate marks and praise differentially in proportion to talent and effort. Respect does not have to be deserved, in this logic, but a reward does.

The domain-specific nature of the underlying criteria of justice applied by pupils is made clear by their minimal support across all countries for the idea that hard-working pupils should be treated better by teachers. Pupils have already agreed that hard work or effort is important in terms of teachers awarding marks. This is not a contradiction. It seems that hard work *should* be rewarded in the marking – slightly more so than quality of work (see above). But in all other respects, hard-working pupils are to be treated the same as others. According to the pupils it is again the teachers who are not observing the domain boundaries, in inequitably generalising their appropriate treatment of talented or hard-working pupils in the domain of marking to other domains relevant to trust, autonomy, and respect perhaps. This is deemed inappropriate.

Table 7.6   Percentage agreeing with statements about how schools should be run

	Belgium (Fr)	Czech Republic	England	France	Italy	Japan
All pupils should be treated with equal respect	94	92	84	93	94	82
Teachers should treat pupils' opinions with respect even if they disagree	94	87	87	93	86	45
Teachers should take care not to humiliate pupils	90	92	80	91	90	38
Teachers should continue explaining until all understand	88	82	81	84	85	50
Pupils' marks should reflect quality of their work	81	91	71	81	84	53
Teachers should praise deserving pupils	81	80	87	82	72	79
Pupils' marks should reflect their effort	73	73	69	77	72	54
Teachers should treat hard-working pupils the best	20	10	27	22	27	26

In order to understand more about the conflicting criteria of justice in play when making decisions about equity, we devised a number of vignettes or small stories that are partially reproduced below (using the names of characters from the English versions). These stories appeared to be particularly useful when dealing with some of the most vulnerable pupils. In the first of these scenarios, pupils were asked to decide between rewarding effort or cleverness in marking an assignment.

Sam spends all evening doing his homework. He researches and writes up his findings using his own words. Pete quickly scribbles down some answers to the homework on the way to school. When the homework is marked, Sam gets a lower grade than Pete.

a) It is not fair that Sam gets a lower mark when he has put in a lot of effort

   b) Pete must be cleverer than Sam, so it is fair that he gets a higher
mark even though he didn't put in as much effort

Pupils in Japan are slightly more in favour of rewarding cleverness
than hard work, while the balance in the EU countries is the reverse
(Table 7.7). This is consistent with the views on what it is that marks
should reward (see above). In Chapter 8 we look at the responses by
groups such as high and low attainers.

The second scenario is:

Jenny's family have a different religion to most people, and they
want Jenny to be taught in a school based on that different religion.
This means that she has will not go to her local school.
   a) This is not fair because school is one place where people who
are different should be able to work alongside each other
   b) This is fair because people who are different should have the
opportunity to attend different schools

In the EU countries a clear majority would prefer that children from
families with different religions mix in the same schools (Table 7.8). In a
sense, the needs for social cohesion outweigh the choices and concerns
of individuals here. A larger minority in England than elsewhere wish
to promote separate schooling for different religions.

Table 7.7 Percentage of pupils agreeing with the first option in the
'Sam' vignette

Belgium (Fr)	Czech Republic	England	France	Italy	Japan
60	60	58	67	65	44

Table 7.8 Percentage of pupils agreeing with the first option in the
'Jenny' vignette

Belgium (Fr)	Czech Republic	England	France	Italy	Japan
79	72	64	77	84	–

Note: This vignette was not included in the instrument for Japan, as it was
considered 'inappropriate' by researchers there.

The third scenario is:

> Jacinta has difficulty reading and finds it hard to keep up in class. The teacher has to spend a lot of time helping Jacinta and gives her a lot of attention. Sometimes the other pupils have to wait for the teacher to stop helping Jacinta and to come and help them.
>   a) Jacinta needs extra help so it is fair that the teacher should spend more time helping her
>   b) The teacher should spend equal time with all the pupils. It is not fair

This is the vignette that provoked the largest disagreement between countries. In four EU countries the majority of pupils used a principle of discrimination, allowing extra help for someone struggling in class. Equal treatment is not fair. But in England and Japan the majority of pupils went for a strict egalitarian response (Table 7.9). The name used in the vignette was deliberately chosen to portray the possibility of a recent immigrant with the home language of the survey as a second language. Since this name was changed in each country we cannot be sure that this implication was equally forceful. Nevertheless the scale of the difference is remarkable, dwarfing anything reported in this chapter so far.

The next two examples involve a three-way choice for pupils.

> If a pupil has difficulty reading and finds it hard to keep up in class, do you think it is fair that
>   a) the teacher spends more time helping this pupil
>   b) this pupil should have to work harder to keep up with the rest of the class
>   c) the pupil is taught in a different class

Again, England and Japan stand out in their responses. Most of the EU country pupils are divided between requesting that a struggling pupil making more effort and a teacher giving more help (Table 7.10).

Table 7.9   Percentage of pupils agreeing with the first option in the 'Jacinta' vignette

Belgium (Fr)	Czech Republic	England	France	Italy	Japan
70	81	39	66	72	30

Table 7.10   Percentage of pupils agreeing with the each option in the extra help vignette

	Belgium (Fr)	Czech Republic	England	France	Italy	Japan
a) Help	42	56	28	49	64	16
b) Effort	51	34	9	39	32	67
c) Separate	5	9	59	8	3	13

In reality of course these approaches are not exclusive. Indeed, support for the teacher giving extra help may be contingent on the pupil being deserving of help by showing that they are making an effort (see responsibility theory in Chapter 5). In England and Japan there is little support for extra teacher attention. This is deemed unfair. Instead, Japanese pupils predominantly support the pupil themselves making more effort. English pupils predominantly support the pupil being taken out of class for extra support. Perhaps this also links to their support for pupils of different religions being taught in separate schools. In England, at least, the comprehensive nature of some learning settings and the inclusive nature of schools in contrast to the widespread retention of special schools in France and elsewhere, might mean that the issue of help for challenged pupils is more real and more time-consuming. It is easier for pupils to agree that others be given extra help in a heavily selective educational setting, for example, because the cost of enforcing that principle will be lower.

The second three-way choice was:

If a pupil is badly behaved in class, do you think it is fair that
a) the teacher gives more attention to this pupil than to other pupils
b) the teacher gives less attention to this pupil than to other pupils
c) the teacher gives the same attention to all pupils

When a pupil is badly behaved (as opposed to struggling) then there is very little support in the EU countries for the teacher giving the culprit extra attention (Table 7.11). Presumably, in this case the attention is neither deserved by the efforts of the pupil nor required to overcome an inherent disadvantage, again in line with responsibility theory (Chapter 5). Most pupils therefore want equal teacher attention and there is even some support for the idea of a badly behaved pupil forfeiting attention.

Table 7.11   Percentage of pupils agreeing with each option in the extra attention vignette

	Belgium (Fr)	Czech Republic	England	France	Italy	Japan
a) More attention	7	19	7	8	16	42
b) Less attention	33	24	39	30	21	6
c) Equal attention	59	56	50	60	62	50

Japan stands out as the country in which a relatively high proportion of pupils think it is fair for the badly behaved to be supported. This could be because pupils in Japan are less likely to have had direct experience of the disruption to lessons that could ensue (a cultural difference perhaps). Or it could be because they are more sensitive to the idea that the bad behaviour is a manifestation of educational disadvantage. If so, the situation is more like that of a pupil struggling to read (see above).

The rather strong views from some of the Japanese pupils, coupled with their awareness of the political and social world outside their own spheres, are an interesting difference to emerge from this part of the study. How these notions are formed, how they manifest themselves in the pupils' activities, and the extent to which they persist would be a very interesting area of future comparative work.

> It will go on forever once we start to count unfairness. What annoys me the most is some specific pupils always escape from being punished because of their excuses, while other pupils have to do some punishments such as cleaning for a week. It is teachers' fault…this unfairness. It seems impossible to change this, but I hope to change. (Japan, male)

In the next chapter we start to look further at how the criteria used to judge educational equity are shaped by the experiences and backgrounds of pupils in all countries. For now, we turn to pupil experiences and views on justice outside schools.

Interaction with parents

Pupils largely report having a positive relationship with their parents, a pattern which was consistent across all six countries (Table 7.12). Parents were considered to be much more likely than teachers to treat pupils' opinions with respect and were just as likely to talk to them about

Table 7.12   Percentage agreeing with statements about parental involvement

	Belgium (Fr)	Czech Republic	England	France	Italy	Japan
My parents are interested in my well-being	91	85	87	88	95	80
My parent treat my opinions with respect	80	70	71	79	71	41
My parents talk to me about school	78	82	80	76	79	62
My parents talk to me about my interests	71	74	74	71	69	60

school as they were about friends and interests. This is true for males and females, and those made to repeat one or more years at school. Among the Japanese pupils, however, only around 40% agreed that their parents treated their opinions with respect (although around one-third of pupils gave a neutral response to this statement). This level of agreement is much lower than that for the EU pupils – over 70% of whom agreed with this statement. Again this may be a cultural difference with parental respect flowing more in one direction than the other.

Views about life outside school

Sadly, most young people have learnt that they need to be very cautious when dealing with adults and other people outside school, and few agree that people can be trusted (Table 7.13). As with several indicators, England and Japan are again similar. Pupils in those countries are more trusting of people in general and less likely to be cautious in dealing with them. Only a minority in all countries trust their own governments to be fair, suggesting that this is an indictment of governments in general.

The figures in the Czech Republic (11%) and Japan (10%) are very low for trust of the government. Indeed, the apparent scepticism of some of these Japanese pupils with regard to their national government is clearly shown in some of their comments:

> The government collects tax from us, but most of the money is spent for personal favours for people in the government, or spent for the U.S. military because of the Japanese-U.S. security treaty. Is it really necessary to spend our money to build wonderful institutions for

the U.S. military, which is not sure whether they will really protect us, and who have taken toll on the Japanese people more and more? The government says, in the media like on TV, that they will use tax for the public. But isn't it unfair to spend money, which our parents earn as a result of their hard work, on the personal purposes of the people in the government? We must study and consider more about this issue at school. School should teach us more about the reality of what happens in Japan and the world. (Japan, female)

Japanese politics is unfair to Japanese people. The politicians take their preferences for their own wealthy and safe life and other people come after that. It is better to sack all the present useless politicians, and employ the honest young ones who are motivated to think of the public. (Japan, male)

Instead of raising the fuel prices, there should be some other ways to save tax. The speed eating contest on TV should be stopped. It is unfair to people, who cannot eat, in poor countries. (Japan, female)

The government officials spend people's tax in vain. There is a big difference between public and private sectors. We cannot participate in government because we are children. We are just watching the nation increasing debt. I am unconvinced. (Japan, male)

Pupils are mostly in favour of immigrants having the same rights as indigenous people in all countries, and a majority also want immigrants to adopt many of the traditions of the new country. Perhaps, in their view, this adopting of 'our way of life' is a condition of having equal rights. In England and Italy (but not Belgium or France), which have had both reasonably high levels of immigration in the last decade and media and policy concern about it, there is less support for equal rights. Pupils in the Czech Republic, where there are few immigrants (see Chapter 6), are the most concerned that new arrivals adopt the cultures and traditions of their new country. At the other extreme are the Japanese pupils among whom only a small proportion (13%) agreed with this. Perhaps the relative homogeneity of Japanese culture can explain this, or perhaps it is based on popular impressions of recent immigration – high skilled U.S. and Chinese workers in Japan and less skilled Gypsy/Romany and ex-Soviet workers in the Czech Republic.

Roughly similar proportions of respondents agreed it was acceptable to hit a person (32% overall) or to tell a lie (27% overall). This is small, but perhaps still too high. All of these patterns are repeated without differentiation for males and females, or those made to repeat one or more

Table 7.13   Percentage of pupils agreeing with statements about life outside school

	Belgium	Czech Republic	England	France	Italy	Japan
I need to be very cautious with people	84	73	51	85	84	33
People coming to live here should have equal rights	71	72	48	71	54	90
I want a professional occupation	66	77	33	57	58	48
People coming to live here should adopt our way of life	53	69	56	58	57	13
I trust my government to be fair	40	11	38	36	28	10
It is OK to lie	36	10	25	32	30	33
It is OK to hit a person	28	50	34	32	26	25
Most people can be trusted	17	20	29	16	11	25

Note: The figures for professional aspiration from England encountered a data entry/coding problem. This indicator is discussed further in Chapter 10.

years at school. In the Czech Republic, the distinction between the two actions was most pronounced, where half of respondents felt that it was acceptable to hit another person, while only 10% agreed that it was permissible to tell a lie.

With regard to young people's experiences of fair treatment outside school, the results tend to be similar across the countries involved. In the next chapter we begin to look at how these views on society emerge from pupils' experiences at school and beyond. But for some pupils at least it is clear that societal justice begins with school justice:

> Teacher's attitudes towards their favourite pupils or pupils who are clever are different from their attitudes towards other pupils. Nowadays people try to get rid of discrimination in society. I am worried about the world if this little discrimination (at school) might recreate discriminations. The politicians also should consider well whether their policies are really right or not. (Japan, male)

8

The Notions of Justice Used by Different Groups of Pupils

Introduction

Chapter 7 looked at pupils' experiences and their judgements about equity in terms of their country of residence. Here we look at some of the same issues in more detail in terms of possible indicators of disadvantage, such as immigration or family socioeconomic status. The chapter works towards a clearer understanding of the criteria of justice used by pupils in practice and appropriate to a variety of settings (see Chapter 5), and of the likely social, familial and educational determinants of those criteria. The ensuing model is then tested in Chapter 10. As in Chapter 7, we supplement the questionnaire results with a selection of open-ended and face-to-face comments provided by young people either on their forms or in discussion afterwards.

The treatment of pupils by teachers

Pupils' reported experiences at the hands of their teachers in school during that academic year, as originally described in Chapter 7, are often surprisingly consistent across social, economic and family background groups. Males, females, high and low attainers, those from families with professional educated parents and those with less educated unemployed parents, recent immigrants and second-language speakers all report pretty much the same experiences. There is almost no noticeable difference in the responses between those made to repeat a year and the rest. The same percentage of each category agreed that their teachers treated them with respect, explained until they understood, encouraged autonomy in learning, generally treated all pupils the same, gave extra help where needed, punished pupils fairly, and marked work fairly. Of course, the situation is not ideal, since the percentage agreeing these things about teachers can often be low, but at least different kinds of pupils are not reporting different levels of agreement. The same lack of variation is noticeable in some less desirable experiences – such as punishments being used unevenly, teachers getting angry with pupils, and teachers having favourites, especially hard-working pupils.

This is also true for many of the other pupil background categories. There is almost no difference, for most indicators, between pupils from families with different occupational and educational histories. Table 8.1, for example, shows around 43% of pupils in all categories agree that teachers tended to respect pupil opinions. The small variation that there is reinforces the message that pupils with potential disadvantages, such as those with parents in lower status jobs, do not report experiencing many forms of potential injustice any more than others do.

Table 8.2, similarly, shows very little variation in response in terms of parental immigration and first language. This is a common finding for most indicators. Here it is clear that pupils moving to the country of the survey after birth are less likely to report teachers getting angry with them. So, for this potentially disadvantaged group in all six countries, there is no special problem in these accounts.

This consistency between most groups of pupils is even greater than between countries. There may be several reasons for this. The

Table 8.1 Percentage of pupils agreeing with statement 'Teachers respected pupil's opinions even if they disagreed with them' – an example of lack of variation between categories

All	Mother 'low status' job	Mother no job	Mother not university	Father 'low status' job	Father no job	Father not university
43	44	43	43	45	43	43

Note: Does not include Japanese pupils.

Table 8.2 Percentage of pupils agreeing with statement 'Teachers got angry with me in front of the whole class' – an example of lack of important variation between categories

All	Moved after birth	Second language	Mother born elsewhere	Father born elsewhere
36	28	39	39	38

Note: Does not include Japanese pupils.

'unconscious victim' thesis, that oppressed people are sometimes less aware of injustice than objectively more favoured, is discussed in Chapter 7. It is found to be insufficient as an explanation for the equal treatment of pupils who might otherwise be considered to be at a disadvantage. The variables we used to form sub-groups such as sex, social class, and so on, might be poor measures of underlying variation but they are standard analytical categories in the sociology of education. We also included in our analysis a wider variety of variables, such as attainment and first language, than is common in sociology traditions. Therefore, our first conclusion is that the experiences of pupils are largely unstratified by their background and origin. In general, for equity, this could be a good finding if equal treatment is the appropriate response to potential disadvantage. At least, schools do not seem to be exacerbating early disadvantage through the interaction of teachers and pupils.

Some indicators show little variation across categories when considered in isolation, but show the same small variation consistently for one category. Pupils who are substantially over-age for the school year are thought to have had to repeat a year – a phenomenon more common in Belgium, France, and Italy than elsewhere. These repeaters report consistently slightly fewer positive experiences at school and slightly more negative ones (Table 8.3). This pattern only appears for the treatment of the individual pupil by the teacher. It does not appear when the same individuals report how other pupils were treated. Similarly for marks, pupils reporting that they received low marks felt that marking by teachers was somewhat less fair than other pupils.

The notion that both punishments and rewards could be allocated unevenly despite similar circumstances was also apparent in the way that many pupils were perceived to be treated. This suggests that whereas teachers may feel justified in treating pupils differently (for example by rewarding improved behaviour or offering additional support for the least, or sometimes more, able pupils) this can sometimes be perceived as being unfair by other pupils. Probably the greatest area of concern among the pupils was about teachers' apparently indiscriminate way of allocating rewards and punishments. Selected comments from the Japanese and English pupils illustrate this point clearly:

I don't like the way that the least intelligent pupils get loads of praise and awards for doing nothing just because they're unintelligent. (England, female)

How the naughty children get more attention and get highly praised when they manage to produce the same amount of work as the rest of the class which they should be doing anyway. (England, female)

I had finished some work and asked my teacher to read it and see if I could improve, but she said 'no' because she was dealing with other pupils who were misbehaving. (England, male)

Some teachers' attitudes towards pupils are different depending on their marks. (Japan, male)

School teachers pressure pupils who have low marks and they give praise to ones who have good marks. (Japan, male)

There is a big difference in teachers' attitudes towards pupils between those who have good marks and those who do not. (Japan, male)

[Pupil] threw a chair at my head I had 8 stitches. He got 2 days internal suspension. I have sworn at a teacher in the past and got a week external suspension. (England, sex unknown)

Table 8.3   Percentage of pupils agreeing with statements about their treatment by teachers

	High marks	Average marks	Low marks	Repeat year
I got along well with my teachers	77	64	46	58
My marks usually reflect the quality of my work	75	59	43	51
My marks usually reflect the effort I made	72	57	43	52
Pupils got the marks they deserved	61	51	41	–
School was a fair place	59	50	38	43
Teachers continued explaining until I understood	58	54	48	–
I trusted my teachers to be fair	53	43	30	37
Teachers got angry with me in front of the whole class	31	36	47	40
I feel as though I am invisible to most teachers	17	22	39	–
I feel discouraged easily	17	23	42	31
School has been a waste of time	5	8	22	15

Note: Marks were self-reported. On the basis of year of birth, pupils born before 1992 in Belgium, France, and Italy have repeated at least one school year.

Most pupil comments were about behaviour, reward, or punishment. Occasionally the pupils' comments were more about academic teaching and learning issues. It seems that it was pupils in the higher-achieving schools who were more likely to comment on perceived unfairness in academic rather than classroom management or behavioural issues, as the extract below illustrates:

> One class was able to give more drafts of a piece of coursework than another in English – this is unfair because the other class is getting more help. (England, female)

Whereas most of the comments that we received related to unequal treatment within the classroom, others revealed core tensions between pupils within some schools:

> Polish pupils don't get told off for starting fights in school but us English do. This is unfair because we are being accused of racism. They should get to their own school and never be allowed near ours. (England, male)

The views of pupils in different types of schools

The English partners were able to collect and collate a substantial amount of official data on the characteristics of the schools in their sample. Using this we classified schools as relatively academically successful – with more than 70% of pupils gaining five or more GCSE grades A* to C in 2006 – and less successful – with fewer than 70% A* to C or their equivalent. The mean was around 70%. The GCSE is a common examination taken by the cohort starting the school year at age 15. All other qualifications are converted into a GCSE equivalent by the Department for Children, Schools and Families (DCSF).

Only around a quarter of the pupils from families with a parent in a professional occupation attended the lower attaining schools, compared with about half of working-class children. However, there were no notable differences in the responses of pupils from the two different types of schools with regard to their experience of fairness, their views on a fair school and on wider social issues. It may be that the lack of substantive difference is caused by an insensitive classification of attainment here. But this finding could also be important in showing, like other findings (see Chapter 10), that experience of justice is not influenced by the type of school attended.

One small difference in opinions came in response to one of the vignettes (see above) and suggested that pupils attending higher attaining schools were more likely to think that it was fair that the teacher should be able to provide extra help to pupils who needed it. Pupils in the lower attaining schools were slightly more likely to report that teachers should spend equal time with everyone. This supports the suggestion made in Chapter 7 that more homogeneous teaching settings lead to greater expressed support for extra help being given to those struggling. Such support comes at very little cost to the individual, when compared to what might happen in a very mixed teaching group including high-ability pupils and also some with the most severe learning challenges.

Next, we classified schools as having relatively high or low levels of pupil poverty. Family poverty was assessed by eligibility for FSM, which is a commonly used measure of deprivation in the United Kingdom. High-poverty schools were deemed to be those with more than 9% of FSM pupils (the mean for the sample). Low-poverty schools had lower than 9% children living in poverty.

Around a quarter of the pupils from families with a parent in a professional occupation attended the higher-poverty schools, compared with about half of working-class children. Again, there were few differences in reports of equity between the two types of schools. Pupils from higher-poverty schools were slightly less likely to report that their school experience had been a fair one, with 24% strongly disagreeing that school was fair, compared with 18% of pupils in low FSM schools.

Finally, we classified schools in terms of the level of control they have over their pupil intake at admission at age 11. Schools in England can be broadly categorised as more or less selective depending on the amount of control they have over their intake. Schools in the sample with some control over their pupil admissions include independent, Foundation, and voluntary-aided. Schools with limited control over admissions include Community (comprehensives) and voluntary-controlled. Again, there were very few differences in the opinions of pupils who attended these different groups of schools. Pupils educated in independent schools were slightly more likely to think that it was fair that teachers spent extra time with pupils who find the work difficult (see above).

The interaction of pupils with other pupils

Although there is more variation between groups of pupils in their responses to their treatment by other pupils than by teachers, there is still almost no variation in several indicators for most background characteristics. Pupils from different family backgrounds, with low attainment, and of different sexes, respond equivalently to questions about being left out, bullied, having something stolen, having good friends, and having friends who are immigrants or low attainers. As with pupil–teacher relationships, the most notable finding is how little stratification there is in pupil–pupil relationships.

For a minority of pupils, school can be a negative experience. Around 12% of pupils felt that they were left out by their peers, while a similar proportion reported being bullied. The number who reported being deliberately hurt by another pupil is slightly higher than this, with around one-quarter of pupils reporting this experience to a certain extent. In addition, around one-third of pupils said they had an item stolen in the current school year. As in Boulton et al. (2009), the minority who report serious issues like bullying tend to have poorer relationships with the teachers. Some pupils used the open response question to describe their experiences of being bullied by other pupils:

> I am not treated fairly for the way I look and dress. I am judged for my music interests also I get bullied for having my own beliefs and rights. This is not right. (England, sex unknown)

> I was bullied by two girls in year 8 and 9, I did tell a teacher and it did stop for a little while but it started again. These girls were bad behaved and known bullies I think they should have been excluded because I wasn't their only victim. (England, female)

> When people gang up on you in big groups. I think this is unfair as this is intimerdating and usually happens because pupils think it's OK to do so. (England, male)

> I am called by a nickname that I do not like. Other people are not called by their nicknames. It is only me who is called like that. (Japan, male)

> One of my friends often hits me, but he is kind to others. It is unfair. (Japan, male)

> Asians cause all the trouble and fights in this school. It will be more peaceful and a better place to be without them. When they get told off Asians just say that teachers are being racist and it gets dropped, not fair. (England, male)

Pupils with low marks, who have repeated a year, or who have moved to the country of the survey after birth, are somewhat more likely to report being left out or bullied. Immigrants, whether first- or second-generation, are more likely to report having a friend at school who also does not come from the country of the survey.

The views of potentially disadvantaged pupils

A recurring theme in the sociology of education is that there are certain groups of young people, defined by social, family, and ethnic background, who are academically less successful in school. At the aggregate level these tend to be pupils from less wealthy homes, or whose families have experiences of unemployment or low waged work, as well as those recently arrived in their country of residence. Here our interest is in the extent to which these academic inequalities might also appear in young peoples' experiences of fair treatment by their teachers, other adults, and by other pupils. With some exceptions, we were unable to obtain background information about the Japanese pupils, therefore this discussion largely relates to the pupils from the five European countries.

As shown in Chapter 6, the majority of pupils taking part in this study were born in the country in which they were now being educated. However, around 5% (9% in Belgium) of pupils in each country identified themselves as having been born elsewhere. Our findings suggest that the experiences of young people who had moved to the country after their birth were generally little different, and sometimes more positive, than the native born. For example, in Belgium 54% of pupils who had moved to the country agreed that school was generally a fair place, compared with 51% of all Belgian pupils. Indeed, in some respects the views of those who had moved after being born were more positive. In the Czech Republic 46% of those who had moved to the country thought that they were treated fairly by their teachers, compared with 29% for all Czech pupils. Similarly, non-native Czech pupils were also more likely to feel their school marks were fair, that punishments were fair, that their teachers respected their views and were interested in their well-being, and they were less likely to feel that their teachers had favourites. This was despite the fact that recent immigrants in the Czech Republic, in particular, were less likely to report that they enjoyed working with others or that they had good friends in school. Immigrant pupils in Italy were also more likely to agree that they had been left out by their peers. Perhaps unsurprisingly, pupils who had moved to each of the countries after they were born reported being much more likely to have friends who were themselves immigrants. For example, 83% of such French pupils said they had friends who did not come from France, compared with 65% of all French pupils. The direction of the pattern was the same for all countries. Similarly, young people who were born outside the country were overwhelmingly more supportive of the statement that 'people coming to live here should have equal rights' and were generally less likely to agree that immigrants should adopt 'our way of life'. Other views regarding their trust of the government, the extent to which is was OK to lie or hit someone, were similar to those of the rest of the population.

Almost 20% of the young people who participated in this study spoke a different language at home to the language of the school and survey, varying from 7% in the Czech Republic to almost 30% of French pupils. Considering their views of fairness allows us a slightly different perspective on the experiences of those young people who may have been born in the country of the survey but might have a different cultural experience outside school. The findings again suggest that the experiences of this group were generally very similar, and slightly more positive, than those of all pupils together. For example, 52% of the English pupils who spoke a language other than English at home responded positively to the statement about school being a fair place, compared with 46% of all English pupils. Where there were differences between the reported experiences between these two groups, it usually came from the responses of bilingual pupils in the Czech Republic. Of these, 42% reported that they thought school was a fair place, compared with 52% of all Czech Republic pupils. However, the numbers of pupils in this country who spoke a language other than Czech at home is small and so the result is treated with caution. The views of this group about the role of parents and society in treating them fairly were, in many regards, also similar to those of all young people in the sample. In comparison with all the pupils from England, those who spoke a language other than English at home were more strongly of the view that people who came to live in Britain ought to have equal rights and were less likely to agree that they would need to adopt a British way of life.

The proportion of parents who were born in the country in which their children were being educated varied from around 30% of the Belgian pupils to less than 10% of those from the Czech Republic and Italy (see Chapter 6). There were few differences between the responses of those young people whose parent(s) were born elsewhere and that of the rest of the sample. For example, in Belgium 53% of pupils whose mother was born outside the country and 51% whose father was born elsewhere agreed that generally speaking, school was a fair place. This is very similar to the figure for all Belgian respondents. In Belgium, France and Italy in particular their views on immigration were similar to those of the pupils who themselves were born outside the test country.

The proportion of the sample whose fathers had no job was relatively small in each country (around 3%). Fathers who had what might be considered to be relatively low status 'working-class' jobs varied from almost one-half of the sample in the Czech Republic and France to less than 20% in England. A higher proportion of mothers had no job, and the distribution of mothers in 'working-class' employment while generally lower than for men, showed similar patterns between the different countries. With regard to the young people whose parents were in lower status jobs or no job at all, our analysis showed that there was little difference between their views on fairness, compared with the whole sample. Where differences did emerge it was generally between the few pupils whose father had no job and the rest of the respondents. The former group tended to report a more negative experience of school. For example, around one-third of this group of Belgian pupils agreed that school was a fair place, in comparison with over half of all other Belgian pupils. Among English pupils the gap between these views was even wider. In all countries, young people whose father did not work appeared to have somewhat less positive relationships with their families, when compared with all respondents. For example, 56% of Belgian pupils whose father did not work agreed that their parents spoke with them about school, compared with 78% of the whole Belgian sample. However only 4% of the Belgian pupils told us that their fathers were out of work, and so the results again ought to be treated with caution. Pupils were asked whether or not either parent had attended university. The responses of those whose parents (either mother or father) were reported as having received no higher education were little different from the rest of the sample.

Respondents were asked to estimate whether or not they usually obtained 'high', 'average' or 'low' marks in school. Around 12% of the sample (ranging from 6% in the Czech Republic and England to 18% in France) told us that the marks they received were usually low. In all five countries, pupils who report that they obtained low marks were less likely to agree that they trusted their teachers to treat them fairly (38% in England, compared with 60% of all English pupils, for example). However, the proportion who say that they were *actually* treated fairly by their teachers is no different from the rest of the sample in each country. Pupils who report that they tend to get low marks were, perhaps understandably, less likely to agree that their marks reflected their effort or the quality of their work. There was also a tendency for them to agree that hard-working pupils were treated the best and that teachers had favourites. In all countries, teachers were reportedly more likely to get angry with this group, less likely to respect their opinion and less likely to help those who needed it. So these pupils were also more inclined to admit that they got discouraged easily.

As we have information on National Curriculum Year 9 tests for most of the English sample, we can also consider the views of those pupils who really do appear to be less academically successful in school, namely those who achieve Level 4 or below in the English assessment. This lower attaining group of pupils were less likely to see school as a fair place and more inclined to agree that school was a waste of time for them. However, they were at least as likely as their peers to think that their teachers treated them fairly (44% compared with 40% for all English pupils). Similarly these lower attaining English pupils also thought that teachers were no more likely to become angry with them in class, and as likely to encourage them to make up their own minds and to mark their work fairly. On the other hand, they were slightly less likely to think that they got along well with their teachers (55%, compared with 63% for all English pupils) and that their teachers were interested in their well-being. On most other questions, there were few differences between the two groups.

Pupils who reported that they had no desire to get a job – although relatively small in number – did present more negative perceptions of school and how they felt they were treated. For example, around one-quarter of the French group with no desire for a job reported that in their view school was a fair place, compared with almost half of all French pupils. However only 38 French pupils in total fell into this 'no aspiration' category and so these findings need to be treated with considerable caution. Indeed, young people from Italy – a country where the largest proportion of respondents said they did not want a job – differed little in their views when compared with the rest of the Italian sample. So perhaps this is not an issue of great consequence (but see Chapter 10).

Boys reported slightly more negative experiences of school than girls on some indicators. For example, 42% of French boys thought they were treated fairly by their teachers, compared with 52% of girls. Similarly, two-thirds of boys in the Czech Republic report that they got along well with their teachers, compared with almost 80% of girls. Male pupils in several countries were slightly more likely to think that hard-working pupils received better treatment, that school was a waste of time and were less inclined to agree that they were treated no differently to their peers. However, any differences in opinions regarding how they or their peers were treated in school by their teachers were not large and were not consistent across countries. For example, similar proportions of boys and girls thought that their school was a fair place, and that teachers respected their views and were interested in their well being. Where there were some differences between the experiences of male and female respondents, it came in their reporting of the relationship between pupils – for example, French boys were much more likely than girls to report that they had been bullied, boys in the Czech Republic were much more likely to report having had an item stolen and boys in all countries were more likely to say that they had been deliberately hurt by another pupil. That the male experience is perhaps more violent than that of the female is also borne out in the responses of pupils from all countries about whether it was acceptable to tell a lie or to hit another person – in each case male pupils were more likely to think that lying or violence was acceptable, the difference being particularly strong with regard to hitting another person. The views of both boys and girls with regard to their relationship with their parents were similar, as were their views on the extent to which they would trust the government.

Views on justice in schools

There is widespread agreement among all young people that teachers should treat all pupils with equal respect, treat their opinions with care, and take care not to humiliate any of them. According to a majority of pupils, teachers should continue explaining until everyone understands a new topic (a threshold criterion of justice). Pupils are happy that teachers discriminate on the basis of effort and quality, and that they use praise for those who deserve it (a meritocratic criterion of justice). However, they are not prepared for teachers to treat hard-working pupils the best, more generally.

One interesting perspective on the data is to examine whether pupils felt that while they were being treated fairly, their peers were not. Any distinction between what happens to them and what happens to others is largely not borne out by the data and varies little between the six countries. Pupils generally report the same experience for themselves as their peers. It is of course, possible that in responding to these questions, pupils were not reading the questions closely and/or were not making any distinctions between what happened to them and what happened to others and so we should regard these findings with some caution.

In terms of marking work in school, there is a strong relationship between experience and ideal (Table 8.4). Pupils felt that marks should reflect the quality of their work, and the experiences of individuals, of pupils in general and what is reportedly wanted in an ideal school are all largely at the same level. Marks can be merited by effort and quality of work. This is quite unlike the issue of the more general favouring of hard-working pupils, which is widely experienced and even more widely disapproved of (also in Table 8.4). While the young people who participated in this study report that hard-working peers were usually treated the best, it is also clear that they feel that this ought not to be the case. Teachers appear to be generalising their preferential treatment of effort in terms of marks (an appropriate domain for this principle) to areas in which hard work should not be an indicator of preferment. One such area could be respect for all pupils. Again, Table 8.4 shows that the experiences of respect reported by individuals for themselves and for other pupils in general are similar, but a long way from what is desired. Respect is a universal principle of justice, whereas reward for effort is contingent. Almost exactly the same picture appears for teacher explanation. There are large discrepancies in the extent to which pupils felt that their opinions ought to be treated with respect and what they report actually happens. Perhaps unsurprisingly, pupils also felt strongly that teachers should ensure that everyone understood a particular topic but their reported experiences suggest that this is not always the case.

Table 8.4 Comparison between actual and desired treatment in school, percentage of pupils agreeing

Pupils' marks should reflect the quality of their work	71
My marks usually reflected the quality of my work	63
Pupils got the marks they deserved	52
Pupils' marks should reflect the effort they made	68
My marks usually reflected the effort I made	63
Hard-working pupils were usually treated the best	79
Teachers should treat hard-working pupils the best	27
Teachers should treat pupils' opinions with respect even when they disagree	87
Teachers treated my opinion with respect even if we disagreed	42
Teachers treated pupils' opinions with respect even if they disagreed	41
Teachers should continue explaining until all pupils understand the topic	82
Teachers continued explaining until I understood the topic	48
Teachers continued explaining until all pupils understood the topic	45

Teachers are reportedly failing in what pupils see as a universal – the right for everyone to understand.

The patterns in each of the six countries are similar, although in broad terms these suggest that the experience of the Italian pupils is slightly more positive, while that of young people from the Czech Republic is more negative.

Pupils with positive experiences of school and home are more likely to agree with the meritocratic principle that marks at school should reflect the quality of the work done (Table 8.5). Our results show that a similar but less complete pattern applies to the principles that marks should reflect the effort made, and that teachers should praise deserving pupils. The differences here are relatively small, but they are consistent. In this table, and those that follow, the results are presented as odds or odds ratios. Odds of 2.00 would show that a pupil with the experience shown in any row in Table 8.5 is twice as likely to report agreement with the principle stated in the right-hand column. Odds of 0.50 would show the reverse situation of being half as likely to agree with the principle. So pupils with positive experiences of school and home, such as pupils being treated with respect, are somewhat more likely to agree that marks should reflect the quality of work. The odds tend to be small here, as the principle is widely agreed, and so few people disagree. However, it is interesting to note that those with experience of the principle tend to

Table 8.5 Odds of pupils agreeing with a meritocratic principle concerning marks

	Pupils' marks should reflect quality of work
My parents are interested in my well-being	1.25
My marks usually reflect the quality of my work	1.22
Pupils got the marks they deserved	1.17
My marks usually reflect the effort I made	1.17
My parents talk to me about school	1.17
Generally achieve high versus low marks	1.15
School was a fair place	1.14
Teachers treated pupils' opinions with respect	1.14
Teachers gave extra help to those who needed it	1.14

Note: In this table the results are presented as odds. The first cell, for example, shows that young people reporting parents interested in their well-being are 1.25 times as likely, as pupils with uninterested parents, to agree that marks at school should reflect quality.

be even more supportive. So most pupils want fair marking, and this is a clearer trend among those that report experiencing it.

Tables 8.6 and 8.7 confirm that principles such as inclusion and demand for respect (and not humiliation) are also more commonly supported by pupils with positive experiences of school and more commonly rejected by those with negative experiences, such as being hurt by another pupil. This result is somewhat surprising, since it might be argued that pupils confronted with injustice should be more likely to feel strongly about the importance of justice. In fact, the reverse appears to be true. However, experience does have some impact in this positively correlated way. Pupils with experience of mixing, and being

Table 8.6   Odds of pupils agreeing with a universal principle about school mix

	School is one place where people can work together
I have good friends in school	1.23
I have a friend who does not come from this country	1.23
My parents are interested in my well-being	1.19
Teachers gave extra help to those who needed it	1.18
Teachers treated pupils' opinions with respect	1.14
School has been a waste of time	0.86
I was deliberately hurt by another pupil	0.77

Table 8.7   Odds of pupils agreeing with universal principles about respect

	Teachers should treat pupils' opinions with respect	Teachers should not humiliate pupils
Teachers continued explaining until all understood	–	1.24
My parents treat my opinions with respect	1.20	1.13
I have good friends in school	1.16	1.15
My parents are interested in my well-being	1.15	–
Teachers treated pupils' opinions with respect	1.14	–

friends, with immigrant pupils are more concerned that school intakes should mix the two in this way.

Those who had experienced teachers giving extra help to other pupils were more likely (odds of 1.16) to be in favour of extra help being given in the relevant vignette (see Chapter 7). Those who had been hurt by another pupil were less in favour of giving extra help (odds of 0.83). Intriguingly, high-attaining pupils, those who had been bullied or hurt at school were more in favour (1.26) of extra attention for the badly behaved in class, while less in favour (0.83) of extra attention for a struggling pupil. Since 'high' attainment is a relative concept, this could be further confirmation of the impact of streaming pupils into homogenous teaching groups where extra help is easier to give without disrupting the progress of others.

In summary, positive experiences of school and home tend to help produce pupils with positive principles of justice at school, who are tolerant, sharing, and inclusive. Negative experiences of school, against some of our expectations, tend to help produce pupils who are prepared to tolerate and countenance these kinds of injustice at school.

The experience of parents and wider society

Pupils largely report having a positive relationship with their parents. As in the study by Raty et al. (2009), parents in all six countries in our much larger study are seen to be mostly concerned with and assisting their childrens' education. Parents were much more likely than teachers to treat pupils' opinions with respect, and were just as likely to talk to them about school as they were about friends and interests. Although pupils were invited to provide their own examples of unfair treatment either at school or elsewhere, the vast majority of comments related to treatment at school – perhaps unsurprisingly because the main focus of the questionnaire had been on school experiences up to that point. The few pupils who chose to comment on their relationships with their families also tended to focus on inconsistent allocation of punishments:

> At home when I did nothing wrong apart from leaving my bag on the floor out of the way and my mum shouted at me for it, when someone else did the same thing but didn't get shouted at for it. (England, male)

> My brother receives the same amount of money as me (from our parents) even though he is three years younger than me. Then he wastes money. (Japan, female)

> When I quarrel with my younger sister, I scold her because she obviously did something wrong. But my parents say that it is my fault. It is not fair. Although she is younger and she is my sister, it is unfair that she, who caused the quarrel is not scolded as much as I am. (Japan, male)

From this small sample, it appears that the same principles of justice apply as at school. Young people are not objecting to the notion of punishment as such. It is a fact of life for some. They object to inconsistency of application and apparent favouritism. Whether this widespread feeling of inconsistency is warranted, or whether it is a consequence of the fact that punishment of the respondent is necessarily more painful than the punishment of others, is not possible to determine with these data. However, it should be noted that in the school context, there is little difference between pupils' reports about themselves and others (see above). If we assume that respondents were sufficiently aware of the difference in the wording of questions, this does suggest that there is some justification to these feelings of unfairness.

There is a consistent relationship between a pupil's relationship with parents and reported experiences at school. These are presented here as odds – the percentage with a good relationship with their parents divided by the percentage of the rest who report each experience with teachers. Some are small (nearer 1) and some are large (nearer 2 or 0.5) but all point in the same direction. Young people who report respectful concerned parents also tend to report positive experiences of school and with teachers (Table 8.8).

Pupils with good relationships with their parents are also less likely to report negative experiences with other pupils, such as being bullied (Table 8.9). We examine whether these are more likely to be parental or background effects, or some other kind of correlation, when we model these associations in rough biographical order for Chapter 10.

Turning to society beyond the family, the comments made by pupils provide a good illustration of how some young people felt that they were treated unfairly by the adults they encounter outside school. Their comments suggest interesting similarities between nations and cultures:

> Outside of school I am treated unfairly in shops, restaurants and most public places when I am with a group of peers. (England, sex unknown)

> I think it is unfair when people of a certain age (i.e., under 16) are not allowed in a shop because 'they cannot be trusted'. I am mature

Table 8.8 Odds of pupils agreeing with statements about their relationship with parents, after positive experiences

	Are interested in my well-being	Treat my opinions with respect	Talk to me about my interests	Talk to me about school
Teachers have been interested in my well-being	1.78	–	1.40	1.45
School was a fair place	1.77	1.32	–	1.46
Teachers continued explaining until all understood	1.58	1.25	1.31	1.40
I have always been treated fairly by my teachers	1.57	1.26	1.26	1.27
I trust my teachers	1.55	1.31	1.34	1.42
Teachers treated pupils' opinions with respect	1.54	1.53	1.29	1.38
Teachers gave extra help to those who needed it	1.49	1.25	1.23	1.30
Teachers punished bad behaviour fairly	1.47	1.29	1.31	1.44
Teachers continued explaining until I understood	1.47	1.24	1.21	1.27
Teachers got angry with me	1.45	–	1.24	1.22
Teachers treated my opinions with respect	1.42	1.47	1.25	1.32
Pupils got the marks they deserved	1.42	1.25	–	1.25
My marks usually reflect the quality of my work	1.35	1.19	1.23	–
I got along well with my teachers	1.34	–	1.25	1.28
Teachers treated me no better or worse	1.33	1.23	–	1.21
My marks usually reflect the effort I made	1.30	1.22	1.22	1.27
I enjoyed working with other pupils	1.21	–	1.21	1.23

Table 8.9   Odds of pupils agreeing with statements about their relationship with parents, after negative experiences

	Are interested in my well-being	Treat my opinions with respect	Talk to me about my interests	Talk to me about school
I feel discouraged easily	0.63	–	–	–
I was left out by other pupils	0.56	–	–	–
I was deliberately hurt	0.55	0.65	–	–
I feel as though I am invisible to pupils	0.54	–	–	–
I was bullied by other pupils	0.53	–	–	–
School has been a waste of time	0.47	–	0.54	0.47

Note: Cells marked '–' have a value judged too close to 1 to repeat – generally below 1.2 or above 0.8.

and reliable and I think I should be allowed to shop where I want. (England, sex unknown)

I passed a middle aged to old woman on my bike. She caught up to me and started shouting towards me and my brother. I believe this showed a lack of respect as she did not know what I am like as a person or academically. She could have made her point, and I would have apologised. The incident was extremely insulting and rude. (England, female)

[It is unfair] when older people consider all teenagers to be 'Yobs' because it isn't our fault we're teenage and not all teenagers are the same. (England, male)

People who deliver leaflets in the town do not give them to us because they think us to be children. Shopkeepers also do not say greetings to us as they do to adult customers. (Japan, female)

The transportation fee for buses and trains for junior high school pupils are higher than those for primary school pupils. The space that we need in the buses and trains is almost the same as for primary school children. (Japan, female)

One distinctive aspect of the responses from the Japanese pupils, particularly when compared with their English peers, is the extent to which their comments referred to the role of government in public life and its implications for society more widely:

> There is a gap between rich and poor people in the world. It is strange that there are people who have difficulty living, while some people spend money on stupid things. (Japan, female)

Views on justice in wider society

How then are pupil background characteristics and their school experiences related to their views on citizenship, ethics, and the role of justice in life beyond the classroom? The overall and national pictures of responses to these items is dealt with in Chapter 7. Other than country of survey the only background characteristic, leading to variation on only one item, was sex of pupil. Boys were 1.78 times as likely as girls to report that it is ok to hit another person if they have insulted your best friend. There is no indication as to why this should be, although boys were also more likely to have been hurt at school. As above, pupils reporting interested and concerned parents were more likely (around 1.25 times) to respond positively about trusting their own government, and trusting most people. They were less likely (around 0.7 times) to respond that it is ok to lie in order to avoid punishment, to hit someone, and that immigrants should adopt the local way of life. Whether these are direct effects, such that pupils nurtured by caring parents are more trusting, or whether these are disguised context effects, is discussed in Chapter 10.

Pupils reporting that they wanted a professional occupation after their education differed in their experiences of and attitudes to school. Perhaps unsurprisingly those reporting higher attainment were more likely to aspire to professional occupations (55%) than average (47%) or low attainers (35%). They are more likely to have good friends at school (1.2), and less likely to have been bullied (0.78) or to see school as a waste of time (0.67).

Experience at school is strongly related to feelings of trust about people more generally (Table 8.10). Those for whom school was fair, and their teachers were just, were nearly twice as likely as others to report trusting the government of their country and most people in general. It seems possible that pupils' experience of school contributes to their image of what wider society will be like (see below). If so, teachers, leaders and

Table 8.10   Odds of pupils agreeing with statements about trust

	I trust my government	Most people can be trusted
I trust my teachers	1.82	1.71
School was a fair place	1.81	1.64
Teachers treated pupils' opinions with respect	1.70	1.38
Teachers punished bad behaviour fairly	1.69	1.38
Teachers gave extra help to those who needed it	1.67	–
All pupils were treated the same way	1.60	1.67
I have good friends in school	–	1.58
Pupils got the marks they deserved	1.57	1.47
I got along well with my teachers	1.55	1.50
Teachers treated my opinion with respect	1.54	–
I have always been treated fairly by my teachers	1.54	–
Teachers continued explaining until all understood	1.52	1.38
Teachers treated me no better or worse	1.52	–
Teachers continued explaining until I understood	1.46	–
I enjoyed working with other pupils	1.43	1.75
My marks usually reflect the quality of my work	1.38	–
Teachers have been interested in my well-being	1.38	1.44
My marks usually reflect the effort I made	1.32	–
School has been a waste of time	0.68	–

policy-makers have a direct responsibility to assist pupils in making positive but appropriately critical judgements. Note that this is not primarily a pedagogical or curriculum issue. Pupils learn about what society is like through their lives at school. Put simply, there is little point in overtly teaching that people can be trusted if pupils are not trusted in schools, and teachers do not behave according to what pupils see as widespread principles of justice. We explore this further in Chapter 10.

There was almost no variation in the experiences of pupils who agreed that immigrants to their country should be given equal rights, or should adopt the local customs, and the rest. In terms of agreeing, conditionally, that it is 'ok' (the term used in the English instrument) to hit someone who has been insulting or lie to avoid punishment, there is considerable variation related to past experiences (Table 8.11). Those pupils reporting serious negative experiences of school such as being hurt, and perhaps less serious but more chronic injustice at the hands of teachers, were considerably more likely to tolerate or even support hitting and lying in turn.

Again, positive school experiences and relationships with teachers are associated with a lower likelihood of agreeing to violence and deception, whereas negative experiences are linked to the more 'negative' view in traditional terms (Table 8.12). These positive experiences

Table 8.11   Odds of pupils agreeing with statements about lying and hurting others, after negative experiences

	It is ok to hit a person	It is ok to lie
School has been a waste of time	2.07	2.08
Teachers got angry with me	1.65	1.36
Teachers had favourite pupils	1.61	1.67
Hard-working pupils were treated the best	1.54	1.72
I feel as though I am invisible to most teachers	–	1.52
Some pupils were punished more than others	1.48	1.63
I was deliberately hurt by another pupil	1.29	1.38

Table 8.12   Odds of pupils agreeing with statements about lying and hurting others, after positive experiences

	It is ok to hit a person	It is ok to lie
Teachers treated me no better or worse	0.76	0.71
Teachers continued explaining until I understood	0.76	–
Teachers gave extra help to those who needed it	0.74	–
I trust my teachers	0.72	0.59
Teachers treated pupils' opinions with respect	0.72	0.72
I have always been treated fairly by my teachers	0.70	0.65
Teachers punished bad behaviour fairly	0.69	0.65
I got along well with my teachers	0.66	0.58
School was a fair place	0.64	0.63
Pupils got the marks they deserved	–	0.73
Teachers continued explaining until all understood	–	0.72
All pupils were treated the same way	–	0.66

are almost exclusively about teachers and the principles of justice that they apply to routine school events like explanation and getting on with pupils. It is reasonable to suggest that teachers have a role in discouraging agreement with violence and deception not just by teaching about it, and not just by displaying their beliefs about violence in their work. Most countries have abolished corporal punishment anyway. Teachers can encourage more positive beliefs about these wider social issues merely by illustrating through their normal everyday teaching behaviour that a just world is possible.

When invited to offer an example of their own experience of unfair treatment, some pupils described instances where they were treated unfairly, both inside school and out, because of their skin colour:

> I was racially abused by my French teacher, also stopped by the police and searched as my skin colour was different. I was not chosen for the football team because of the way I look. (England, male)
>
> I was racially abused by a police officer, it's against the law. He said I should go back to my country and he also said I was brown. I took as a very big insult. (England, male)

What is life at school like for a high-profile minority of pupils, often recent immigrants, who are of Muslim background?

Recent immigrants from countries with high Muslim populations

An issue of current concern within the EU and further afield is the education of the minority of Muslim young people, mostly arising not from conversion but through repeated periods of immigration. We included a question on pupil family religion in the pilot study, but did not find that it worked well. Thus, we do not know the religion of pupils in the main study, but it is still of interest to consider briefly the experiences of recent immigrants from countries with a high Muslim population. There are 732 pupils in the five EU countries who had been born in, or who had at least one parent born in, a predominantly Muslim country – mostly Morocco, Algeria, Turkey, and Pakistan. Of course, many of these may not be Muslim, and some Muslims will originate elsewhere, including in the test countries. Most are second-generation immigrants living in France (399). None were from the Czech Republic. It is important to recall also that the pattern of immigration to each of the other four countries has been very different socially and historically. Those arriving in England have tended to come from Commonwealth countries, including some professional families moving from Kenya and Uganda, whereas immigration in mainland Europe has been more from North Africa, the Middle-East, and more recently from Eastern Europe. Perhaps this also relates to differences in educational background. In England, for example, 60% of recent immigrants from Muslim countries report at least one parent who had a university education compared to 43% nationally. In Belgium, on the other hand, only 40% of immigrants from Muslim countries have a parent with a degree compared to 50% nationally.

There was no difference between the reported support and interest of the parents of recent immigrant and other pupils. Two-thirds of recent immigrants from Muslim countries and of pupils overall agree that they get along well with their teachers. At school, recent immigrants from Muslim countries report very similar levels of interactions with other pupils as the overall figures. Around 10% report violence from other pupils at school, and around 5% have had something stolen. Similarly, recent immigrants do not feel more left out by other pupils than the overall figures (around 10%); they do not report feeling any more invisible (around 7%). Most of them have good friends in school (more than 90%) and generally enjoy working with others (75%). Immigrants from Muslim countries more often (78% versus 56%) reported having friends who were also recent immigrants, perhaps reflecting the makeup of the schools they attend, or the areas in which they live. In Belgium, Italy and England there was generally no difference in the reports of equity in dealing with teachers between immigrants from Muslim countries and others. However, in France, 27% of Muslim pupils compared to 20% of mainstream pupils found school to be generally unfair.

About one-third of recent immigrants from Muslim countries (32%) do not trust their teachers to be fair, whereas the overall figure for other pupils is lower (23%). Again, however, almost all of these differences are accounted for by the French respondents, among whom 41% of immigrant and 30% of other pupils do not trust their teachers to be fair. In Belgium the figures are 31% and 27%, in Italy 23% and 22%, while in England the recent immigrants from Muslim countries are slightly more trusting of their teachers than the other pupils are. These differences are, reportedly, due to differences in treatment by teachers. Again, immigrants pupils more often report not always being treated fairly by their own teachers, especially in Italy (30% versus 21% overall) and France (31% versus 25%) with no difference between reports in England. In Belgium, Italy and France the immigrants from Muslim countries are considerably more likely to report having been told off by a teacher in front of the whole class (humiliation) – Belgium (40% vs. 32%), Italy (36% vs. 25%) and France (47% vs. 34%). Again, no difference was reported in England.

In our small sub-sample, the mothers of recent immigrants from Muslim countries have similar occupational profiles to other pupils, but their fathers are more predominantly working-class (50% compared to 35% overall). Of course, part of this difference could be accounted for by the phenomenon of a submerged middle class, sometimes observed with patterns of inter-continental emigration. As illustrated in Chapter 10, the professional status of pupils' parents is important – the higher the occupational status of mother or father, the higher the aspirations of their children tend to be, *ceteris paribus*. Thus, we might expect recent immigrants to be slightly less aspirational than other pupils, but in fact the reverse is so. There is also no difference between groups in terms of those who do not want to work at all – sometimes taken as characteristic of low aspiration in a 'culture of poverty' among immigrant and minority groups who are poorly integrated. There is no difference here in aspirations of boys and girls from Muslim countries, a fact which does not support other studies claiming that there will be cultural differences (Heitmeyer and Legge 2008).

Pupils usually do not have high levels of trust in their governments, in adults other than their parents, and in society in general. Recent immigrants from Muslim countries tend to have slightly higher levels of trust, more so among girls (Table 8.13). Again, however, the situation is reversed in France where 38% of immigrants do not trust their government compared to 25% overall. This may have been the result of one or two high-profile policies enacted in French schools from 2005 on,

Table 8.13 Percentage of pupils agreeing with statements about wider society

	Immigrant	Other
People who come to live to this country should have the same rights as everybody else	84	58
I must be very cautious when dealing with other people	81	76
People who come to live to this country should adapt to its way of life	39	59
The government treats people fairly	39	34
It is ok to hit someone	37	29
I trust most of people	23	17

such as the banning of conspicuous religious dress or symbols. This was meant to be an egalitarian measure, based on an equal treatment principle of universal application. But at least some commentators saw it as an inequitable measure, using for themselves either an individualist justification, or another universal principle – autonomy. On the other hand, these media-inflamed issues may reflect a deeper injustice, in the treatment and behaviour of minorities, in French schools.

Recent immigrants from Muslim countries are more likely to report agreeing that it is ok to hit someone, and 39% (compared to 29% overall) agree that it is ok to lie to avoid being punished. It is not clear from these data whether this is an anomaly caused by small numbers, an issue of integration, or to do with their experiences of injustice. Perhaps unsurprisingly, immigrants from Muslim countries are more likely (85%) to want the same rights for new immigrants, compared to others (58%). This is especially so in France and Belgium. The clear majority of most pupils believe that recent immigrants should adapt to the way of life of their new country, but only around one-third of immigrants agree. Otherwise and in general insofar as these cases represent the views of at least some Muslims, recent immigrants want the same opportunities and treatment as everyone else.

Summary

The majority of pupils who participated in this study report that they generally had a positive relationship with their teachers, and that their teachers tended to treat them fairly. The pedagogic relationship was also relatively positive. Most pupils reported that their teachers rewarded their efforts fairly and many had their opinions treated with respect. While the majority of pupils report that their experiences of school are largely fair, there were nevertheless large numbers who disagreed. It was not the case that all pupils felt that they were treated fairly or with respect by their teacher or that their teachers were interested in their well-being. As seen in Chapter 7, Italian pupils generally reported having the most positive experiences and pupils from the Czech Republic the most negative. One of the clearest areas of concern was their perception that teachers treated certain groups of pupils differently and were inconsistent in their allocation of rewards and punishments. The vast majority of pupils were aware that their teachers had pupils whom they favoured, in particular those perceived to be hard-working. This was borne out by their open-ended comments. The English pupils, in particular, were concerned about the unequal attention that teachers gave to different groups of pupils in class. Their comments spanned a range of different pupil characteristics from the badly behaved, to the lower attainers to the more academically successful – with the consensus being that teachers ought to treat all pupils in the same way in most respects.

Of particular interest in this study were the experiences of those young people who were considered to be the most vulnerable, such as those from less wealthy homes, recent immigrants and the academically less successful. That their experiences of school might not be as fair as that of their peers is summed up by one of the English respondents when asked to report any instances when they had been treated unfairly: 'Personally no! As I am Caucasian middle class and well-spoken. If I was not however, this section might be rather different'. However, examining the responses of those pupils who comprise these more vulnerable groups suggests that their experiences of fair treatment are *not* appreciably more negative than their peers. For example, the responses of non-native pupils or those who had different cultural experiences at home (in terms of the language they spoke) were similar to their peers. With regard to attainment, pupils who told us that they tended to be graded at lower attainment levels reported somewhat more negative experiences of school. However, for the English sample, we were able to consider their actual attainment in Key Stage 3 assessments. This suggested that pupils who were achieving at the lower National Curriculum Levels (Levels 3 or 4) did not report that their school experience was less fair than that of their peers.

What about young people experiencing unequal but special treatment through being educated outside mainstream schools?

Part V
Putting It All Together

9
The Experiences of Pupils Educated Otherwise

Introduction

This chapter summarises the case study research we undertook with young people whose educational experiences make them potentially among the most marginalised in society. This work was undertaken with groups of young people in the French-speaking Community of Belgium and in England. These are pupils who, for a range of educational, social, medical and emotional reasons, are educated separately from the majority of young people in our schools. Precisely because of this, an understanding of *their* experiences of being treated fairly is crucial to our research in this area.

The inclusion (or exclusion) of young people with SEN in mainstream schools is an area of international research and policy interest (Opp 2007, Shamir 2007, Thomas and Loxley 2007). From a social justice perspective, advocates of inclusion argue that separating pupils on the basis of education need is no different to what are now illegal minority group segregation practices, in terms of race perhaps. Others point to the limitations of the mainstream classroom and argue for the tailored support and instruction that is available to young people through specialised provision (Ferguson 2008). The situation we are presented with is paradoxical. On the one hand special schools offer support and pedagogical approaches that effectively, efficiently and directly address their pupils' needs. But on the other, these pupils are taught on the margins of their peers' society, a situation which may ill prepare them for life as integrated citizens.

The inclusion debate has traditionally been over *where* pupils were educated. But what are the educational experiences of those young people with special educational needs who are now educated in mainstream schools (often in discrete groups) and of those who remain in the special schools? According to Lewis et al. (2006), the voices of these young people are rarely heard and what little research exists tends to focus on the retrospective accounts of those who have left education. Research suggests that young people with disabilities are well able to engage in thoughtful discussions about their educational experiences and value their place as engaged contributors to their school communities (De Schauwer et al. 2009). As with their mainstream peers, the difficulty of capturing the voice of disabled pupils is not to be underestimated (Lewis 2004, Tangen 2008). Notwithstanding the 'outsider' perspective which research of this nature necessarily affords, there are also specific ethical, methodological and practical issues, as well as the need to respect these (and of course, other) young peoples' right to silence. While many of these issues are always germane, researching pupils who are likely to have difficulty in expressing their ideas verbally presents additional challenges, both methodological and conceptual (Norwich and Kelly 2004).

The language that we use to describe these young people and their experiences of school can be complex and sensitive. For example, in the United Kingdom it is no longer usual to describe a young person as being 'handicapped', whereas even after translation into English this is a term which is understood and used by our project partners, and presumably by some readers. Therefore, we have decided to retain the use of the word 'handicapped' in the section describing the analysis prepared by our Belgian partners but with the recognition of the caveats attached to its use in certain contexts. We begin by summarising the views of young people who are educated outside mainstream schools in the French Community of Belgium.

The French Community of Belgium

The French Community of Belgium has a well developed system of provision for young people with special educational needs. Currently there are eight different types of provision each catering for a range of specific needs, including young people with medical and learning difficulties as well as those who have been excluded from mainstream provision because of truancy, violence, and so on. However, a consensus over the need to integrate these pupils in mainstream schools is growing. There are obvious practical, pedagogic, social, and psychological difficulties which accompany the effective integration of young people who, for whatever reason, have hitherto been taught outside the mainstream system.

This case study focuses on young people in six different learning environments. A reduced version of the main pupil questionnaire was developed as the basis for data collection. This allowed us to maintain the most substantial items from the main questionnaire which were redrafted as appropriate to the learning needs of the sample. Alongside this simplified version of the main questionnaire we were also able to adapt our data collection techniques to suit the circumstances of the young people who were participating (Table 9.1). The schools which participated in this study were chosen to represent the diverse range of learning environments that exist in the French Community of Belgium. The 36 pupils who were included in this part were aged between 14 and 19 years old. Most of them were born in Belgium (25 from the 29 for whom we have data) and some spoke a language other than the language of the survey at home (7 from the 29).

While undertaking the fieldwork for this phase of the study, working with classroom teachers was essential in order to adapt the methods

Table 9.1   The Belgian sample for young people educated otherwise

Setting	Number of pupils	Instrument used
Special vocational education for girls (mild to moderate 'mental handicap')	5	Shortened questionnaire (read with pupils) + help for writing if necessary + discussions with all the group
Special vocational education for boys (mild to moderate 'mental handicap')	7	Shortened questionnaire (read with pupils) + help for writing if necessary
Special secondary education for deaf and hard of hearing	4	Shortened questionnaire translated into sign language + help for writing if necessary
Special secondary education ('backwardness')	6	Shortened questionnaire + help for writing if necessary + discussions with all the group
School for ill or hospitalized teenagers + one pupil in a host family	8	Complete questionnaire administered by the teacher or by post
Service of school assistance (pupils who excluded from school)	6	Shortened questionnaire + individual interviews
Total number of pupils	36	–

of collecting the data. For example, in the questionnaire items a number of the pupils did not understand the nuances between 'I strongly agree' and 'I agree', or 'I disagree' and 'I strongly disagree'. Some pupils were also better able to respond to the three vignettes which presented examples of actual experiences, as opposed to the questions which were more abstract in nature.

In general our findings suggest that respondents in non-school settings did not indicate that they felt that their experience of schooling was unfair. Rather the results show that the particular form of specialised education which the pupils were experiencing was well adapted for their (and their peers') needs. For example, their teachers helped them whenever they didn't understand; indeed, the item 'Teachers continued explaining until I understood the topic' was agreed with by almost all the young people.

Some pupils, with the relevant knowledge, clearly and positively distinguished between their experiences in special schools and what they had experienced in ordinary education: 'Justice in the schools where I've been is rotten except in hospital'. This might suggest that these pupils have been particularly sensitive to the inequitable situations they have encountered. This finding is of particular concern and is similar to some stories we encountered in the main sample arguing slightly against inclusion for some young people. Pupils with disrupted episodes of schooling were the most critical of issues of (in)justice in mainstream education, which they themselves have tended to reject (see Chapter 8).

As with the main sample, our final question was to ask pupils to write (or otherwise relate) something about their own experiences of fairness (or unfairness) in school, at home or in the community. For some pupils, this was a difficult task, both because of difficulties with expressing their ideas cohoerently but also because of the sensitive nature of the topic: 'Because I don't want to answer. I don't want to tell what happened to me in my family some years ago. Now it's OK. It happened with my uncle. I stop.' Where pupils did feel able to respond, their experiences were similar to those of the 'mainstream' sample and did not appear to draw directly upon their own personal disabilities/ difficulties. Instead they reflected injustices at home: 'My father drinks everyday and there are lots of quarrels', at school 'He was the one upsetting me and I was the one punished', and in wider society, for example about street cleanliness or fines for being 'badly parked'.

Despite the small number of respondents here, and the fact that there are also young people living in difficult situations within ordinary schools, our results suggest that, in Belgium at least, one can think of special education and marginal schooling organisations as places where the pupils felt that they were respected and where their differences were taken care of.

The experiences of marginalised young people in England

This section summarises the results of the equivalent case study research with 66 young people in England. The English case studies focused on the following four groups of pupils:

- Group 1: Home educated (3 siblings from the same family)
- Group 2: pupils identified as having Special Educational Needs and educated within mainstream schools (43 pupils from 10 schools)
- Group 3: pupils identified as having Special Educational Needs and educated in a Special school (4 pupils from 1 school)
- Group 4: pupils identified as having Emotional and Behavioural difficulties educated in two Pupil Referral Units (16 pupils)

Many of the young people had, at some point, attended mainstream schooling, but also experienced a range of difficulties including visual impairment, and mild to severe learning and behavioural difficulties. Some of these young people had been reasonably academically successful in school. It is, therefore, difficult to generalise the results from the case studies on the basis of any single shared characteristic. The young people educated in mainstream schools were particularly diverse, their inclusion in the case study sample was optional and therefore the criteria for their inclusion varied between schools. What these pupils have in common is that in some sense they are different from the majority of their peers. This difference may be a result of an unsuccessful school experience which led to them being excluded from mainstream provision (either by being home-schooled or educated in a Pupil Referral Unit), or the consequence of a particular physical, behavioural, or learning difficulty. As with the case study research undertaken in the French Community of Belgium, the data collection methods adopted for the English case studies involved a mixture of interviews and questionnaire surveys. Three different versions of the main school questionnaire were developed for use in the case study schools.

The following section presents an overview of the findings from this part of the study. Because of the relatively small numbers of young people in each of the four case study groups, their responses are treated together and comparisons are drawn with their mainstream-educated peers who participated in the main sample.

Relationship with teachers

Pupils involved in the case studies tended to have generally positive experiences of school or education otherwise, even when compared with their 'mainstream' peers. For example, well over half of the case study pupils felt that they have always been treated fairly by their teachers and a similar proportion felt that their teachers care about them. Indeed, while the majority of all pupils in the main study felt that they got along well with their teachers, this was a view that was particularly strong among the case study pupils with around 70% either agreeing or strongly agreeing with the statement. Case study pupils were also more likely to feel that their teachers continued explaining until they understood the topic. Over 60% responded positively to this statement, compared with around 48% of the main sample.

However, in the same way as their 'mainstream' peers, some of the case study pupils could point to incidents where they felt that their treatment by their teachers was less than fair. Consider, for example, the following exchange between the researcher and a pupil in the Special School:

> *Mary*: Once I was called a liar.
> *Researcher*: OK, so where did that happen?
> *Mary*: At Don's Farm in [place name].
> *Researcher*: And so who said that to you?
> *Mary*: [name of person] one of the staff here.
> *Researcher*: So you were there on a school trip, were you?
> *Mary*: Yeah and I come back and I talked to [deputy head] and [head] about it and then at lunchtime she came up to me and called me a liar and I thought I was treated unfair then.
> *Researcher*: And how did that make you feel at the time?
> *Mary*: Quite cross because someone shouldn't of jumped on me in the first place.

Where pupils did report incidents where they felt that they had been treated unfairly, their comments reflected the same concerns as their 'mainstream' peers. For example, the issues included the restrictions of school uniform or concerns about the perceived unequal treatment by teachers:

> I think that it is really unfair where the school does not allow 4 pairs of earrings or different hair colour, it's not going to affect our learning.
> I think it is unfair when the teacher will shout at me and not the other girls. Because the teacher don't like us so the teacher treats you unfairly.

Only two pupils reported an incident where the perceived unfairness was related to their special educational need, such as:

> I need help with my reading but never got it.

The following exchange was with one of the home-schooled pupils who was also visually impaired:

> A: [name of previous school] I was not treated fairly because of my disability. … I felt like I didn't enjoy school … and when I have been treated fairly I find I'm a really happy person but when I haven't been treated fairly I feel upset …
> *Researcher*: what did people do that made you feel you were being treated unfairly?
> A: I knew immediately that if I didn't have bad eyes I would have been treated the same as any other pupil but because I have I am treated differently … sometimes in a good way but most of the time in a bad way.

The three home-schooled pupils who participated in this study had somewhat different backgrounds to the rest of the case study pupils. Their self-reported parental occupations suggest that they were from professional backgrounds, whereas the parental occupations of the other pupils would suggest that they were overwhelmingly working-class. Although the previously home-schooled pupils were now feeling reasonably settled and happy at school, they had undergone periods of substantial change in their schooling following periods of unhappiness and repeated incidents of bullying. This resulted in all three girls being educated at home for a period of about 2.5 years, ending approximately 18 months ago. In the interviews with these young people, it became apparent that in addition to their relationships with their peers and their perception of the ways in which teachers dealt with discipline issues, they were also pre-occupied with perceived unfairness in the way teachers treated them with regard to academic work:

> I've always wished that I could be in a school where people thought the same way as me but differently, where they thought for themselves basically, had their own opinions and we would talk about those opinions … and the whole thing like with English … because the majority of the school is foreign, like with culture … so their English is a little bit on the rocks and it makes English lessons difficult because you say something even slightly too advanced for them … but the teacher then has to take 5 minutes to explain to everyone what it actually means. So generally I don't bother to voice my opinions using big words, I put it all down on paper and then the teacher gets surprised when on paper I sound different to who I am in the class … it can get interpreted in different ways, like are you cheating? Have you constantly got a thesaurus with you? Have you copied it off the internet or an older brother or sister? And it gets annoying if the teacher doesn't actually know you … I don't want to sound like I am showing off … as the posh white girl who knows all the big words … I don't want to upset people … be a nuisance … but that can be my downfall.

And with regard to coursework deadlines:

> When you're home-schooled you can prioritise things, at school because it's so structured and scheduled it's difficult to prioritise things because there's deadlines and lessons and stuff. In my year we have science coursework to finish but we can't take that out of school because of cheating … people using the internet … it's difficult because your English teacher is telling you to prioritise English homework but your Science homework you can't take home and the deadline is like tomorrow or something. It would be nice if for a couple of weeks they sort out the timetable so they can prioritise it and sort it all out so that it's not the teacher setting the deadline but the school setting the deadline so it all links in together so that you are not stressing out about coursework. … It is important to have deadlines but they move them … we were told it was Friday and then I still don't understand what I'm doing …

Researcher: So are deadlines helpful?

No because they change so much.…In English I always meet the deadline…but then I can't improve it up to the deadline [following feedback from the teacher] because I've already done it.…I can't get my marks until the rest of the class have done it.…I submitted some coursework before the summer and only got my mark back last week – I was really proud of that work – but that was so annoying…if they gave me my mark early then I could improve on it.

Relationship with peers

Unlike the sample of pupils in the study by Norwich and Kelly (2004) study, the case study pupils were no more likely than the rest to report experiencing bullying or feeling left out by other pupils. The vast majority reported having good friends in school and enjoying working with other pupils.

> A: My school is like a big family. I've got friends in Year 11 and the only sad thing is that they'll be leaving next year…we don't care about year groups. (girl, home-schooled)

However, there were also incidents where pupils had experienced bullying and racist abuse:

> Well people used to be racist so I reacted and I got kicked out of school. (boy, Pupil Referral Unit)

In the Special School, one of the pupils described what happens if she experienced incidents of bullying:

> *Researcher*: And you said you had been bullied by other pupils – do you want to say a bit more about that?
> *M*: Pupils swearing at me…that's not very nice.
> *Researcher*: And what happens here when that kind of thing happens?
> *M*: [head teacher] and [deputy head] gets told straight away.
> *Researcher*: So it sounds like…that [head] and [deputy head] have been involved, so does that mean you feel comfortable about approaching them?
> *M*: Yeah…I think it's quite easy to do [talk to them] because [they] give me more support than ever and that's brung [*sic*] me forward instead of going backwards.

Experience of fairness outside school

In common with the 'mainstream' sample, the case study pupils tended to have positive relationships with their family, and felt that parents/guardians were interested in their well-being. With regard to their wider social experience, the case study pupils were actually more positive than the 'mainstream' sample in their view that most people could be trusted.

The interviews gave us the opportunity to explore young people's experiences of unfairness in more depth than afforded by the questionnaire and enabled this exchange with one of the pupils in the Special School:

> *M*: Yeah and I'm also on the [place name] Youth Council.
> *Researcher*: Do you want to tell me a bit about it?
> *M*: Oh that is so amazing! We are raising money for the hydro sense pool for our school here, we raised £200 and we did a big pop group type thing.
> *Researcher*: Brilliant and so who else is on that council with you?
> *M*: Nobody from this school. Some pupils from different kinds of schools but soon I'm going to have a friend that's gonna come with me so I don't get left out without a friend.
> *Researcher*: OK, and so what does that mean for you in terms of being treated fairly? Is it somewhere you are treated fairly or not?
> *M*: In between sometimes.
> *Researcher*: Why is that?
> *M*: Because I put in for the youth opportunities fund for the school for the swimming pool and I didn't know the date was out so I sent it to them and they said sorry it's too late!

Pupils' views on what a school ought to be like

The case study pupils were presented with three vignettes or scenarios that were very similar to those given to the 'mainstream' group. Once again their views were similar to those of the mainstream pupils. They felt that ability should not be rewarded over effort and that the teacher should spend equal time with all pupils and that it was unfair that pupils had to wait for help. However when asked whether a badly behaved pupil should be given more or less attention, their responses were quite different from the mainstream group. As we can see in response to the scenario below, 40% of the case study pupils thought the teacher should give more attention to the badly behaved pupil, compared with only 7% of the main sample (Table 9.2).

Table 9.2 Percentage of pupils agreeing to extra help for badly behaved pupils

	Mainstream' sample	Case study sample
More help	7	40
Less help	41	21
Same help	52	40

This result is surprising, considering that a similar question concerning a pupil who had difficulty reading did not provoke a similar response. One possible explanation for this surprising result is that the wording of the question was slightly different in both versions. In particular in the mainstream version the word 'attention' was used while in the case study questionnaire this was replaced by the word 'help'. Either way, these young people were generally more tolerant of bad behaviour than their mainstream peers.

The following extracts from the interviews with the three home-schooled pupils illustrate their perspective on what a fair school ought to look like:

> That the pupils are treated with respect and that they are not segregated or singled out because of their height, hair colour or whatever. (female, home-schooled)

> Equal rights and respect, like pupils do argue 'I know my rights' but they should be aware of teachers' rights too. They should be aware that if you do something wrong you should accept you've done something wrong and should be punished for it but then again sometimes, some teachers do take advantage of the fact that they can keep pupils in at lunchtime. There should be an awareness of equal respect and other people's rights 'cause it can't just be 'oh I know my rights' – you need to know them and understand them. (female, home-schooled)

> Have punishments following through and if you do something to one child you should do it to the other, like if someone does something wrong and another person does the same things, make sure that they both get punished in the same way. (female, home-schooled)

Summary

Although the number of case study pupils was relatively small and very diverse, their responses to our questions do suggest that their experience of school is positive and differs little from that of their 'mainstream' peers. For an education system which is perennially concerned with issues of inclusion, these results ought to be considered positively. However, the direct implications of these findings for the inclusion debate are somewhat limited. The sample is small, and coverage of the many diverse groups of vulnerable young people only cursory. Nevertheless, there is good news that pupils educated otherwise report no special problems.

10
Identifying the Determinants of Justice

Introduction

In this chapter we take all of the associations and variations discussed in Chapters 7–9, and try to create explanatory models for at least some of the criteria of justice identified by young people in this study. Our survey variables can be classified in terms of pupil characteristics (e.g., sex), family interactions (e.g., relationship with parents), predictors (e.g., experience of injustice at school), and potential outcome variables (e.g., sense of justice). This enables 'prediction' of the outcome variables using the personal, background and experience variables to assess the influence of family and school on pupils' developing sense of justice.

The models presented here are derived from logistic regression analysis with binary 'dependent' variables – such as professional aspiration, trust, help for the disadvantaged, and whether pupils found school fair. In each case, around 50% of pupils were in each category (such as whether they were willing for a pupil with difficulties to receive extra help at their expense or not). And in each case the regression analysis used the other 'independent' variables to predict which category a pupil would have chosen, so increasing the accuracy from near 50% to perhaps 70% or more (so explaining 40% of the residual variation). Independent variables were entered in four blocks representing pupil background (such as parental occupation), aggregated background (e.g., school-level summaries of parental occupation), parental support (such as whether parents talked to children about schooling), and experience of justice at school (such as whether pupils were bullied). Each stage can only take up and try to explain any variation in outcomes that is left unexplained by an earlier stage. The stages represent a rough biographical order, and so protect the analysis from the invalid influence of later

Table 10.1   Percentage of pupils correctly identified as willing to help criterion or not, by batch of variables

Batch	Percentage predicted correctly	Percentage of remaining variation explained
Base figure	52	–
Pupil background	61	19
Aggregated background	62	2
Parental support	62	0
Experience of justice at school	69	15
Total	–	36

Note: For comparison purposes, we used the same variables to 'predict' an entirely random binary outcome, with a 52:48 split, to assess the dangers of fitting any such model *post hoc*. The best such model using all available 'predictors' is around 54% correct. This means that a lot of the additional variance explained in tables like this is unlikely to be spurious.

proxies (such as success at school replacing parental education). As with all such models, they do not represent any kind of definitive test but are a way of filtering the results to see potential patterns. However, as noted in Table 10.1, we did run alternative models to test the validity of those models we present here. These, along with our inability to predict some other potential outcomes to those discussed here with equivalent success, suggest that the models presented here can bring order to the results in Chapters 7–9, and help to partition the possible impact of background, parent, school, teachers, and other pupils. We start with outcomes related to school.

Predicting one criterion of justice

Whether or not teachers should give more help to a pupil with reading difficulty (even at the expense of the respondent) was used as the dependent variable in a binary logistic regression. In total, 52% of pupils reported that the teacher should give extra help to a pupil with a specific difficulty. The remaining 48% mostly reported that all pupils should have equal attention. In this case, therefore, pupils are almost evenly split about a crucial issue for equity – is help given in class fairer when evenly distributed like respect or when it is given according to need? Any attempt to predict an individual pupil who is happy for more help to be given to another pupil with a difficulty would be 52% correct simply by assuming that everyone was happy with it. The success of our model must be judged on its ability to improve on this baseline figure. The percentage predicted correctly for each stage of the model is in Table 10.1. The model increases the accuracy of prediction, compared to the baseline, by 36% of the otherwise unexplained variation in responses. Of this increase, more than half is attributable to the pupil background, and just under half to experiences at school. There is only a small school mix effect, and most of the variation explained operates at the individual level.

Insofar as we can explain pupil willingness for others to get extra help, pupil background is a major factor. Nevertheless, the sex, attainment, and country of origin of the pupil are irrelevant to this criterion of justice. Also irrelevant are the occupations, education and country of origin of parents. Those living in England are more likely to approve of help given to others than those in Belgium, Czech Republic, France and Italy. This is illustrated in the percentages agreeing with extra help, when this variable is looked at in isolation. The raw figures are England (72%), Belgium (59%), Czech Republic (44%), France (51%), and Italy (36%). In addition, given that the vignette used to pose the question is about difficulty in reading, it is interesting that those not speaking the language of the survey country are generally happier for a pupil struggling with reading to be given extra help (1.26).

There is only a tiny improvement in correct predictions if the pupil background variables are aggregated to the school level as an estimate of the school mix effect of clustering similar pupils in schools and classes. Schools with higher proportions of pupils born in the survey country are less likely to be happy with extra help given to others. Support for the criterion declines by 0.99 for every percentage point of indigenous pupils. The survey included four questions about the pupil's relationship with parents. Using these variables at individual or school level makes no difference at all to the quality of the prediction.

A large number of school experience variables are not relevant to increasing the quality of the prediction, including whether a pupil repeats a year or more (i.e., born before 1991). But there is a very clear relationship, once the preceding factors such as pupil background are accounted for, between pupils' reports of justice in school and their willingness for a pupil in difficulty to receive extra help.

Being respected by teachers, with teachers not getting angry in front of others, not punishing pupils unfairly, concerned for pupil well-being and prepared to explain until everyone understands, are key to pupils being prepared to support help for those with difficulties (or reporting this at least). Taken at face value this suggests a clear role for teachers

Table 10.2 Coefficients for pupil/school experience variables
and willingness to help or not

I have good friends in school	1.70
Teachers were interested in my well-being	1.27
Teachers got angry with a pupil	0.81

Note: All coefficients are in relation to the strongly disagree category. In some ways this table and those that follow are similar to the odds tables presented in Chapters 7 and 8. The main difference here is that these determinants have been modelled to be free of, after taking into account, family and pupil background variables.

in educating citizens who are tolerant and supportive of the difficulties of others (Table 10.2). They do this not only (or perhaps at all) through citizenship pedagogy but through their exemplification of good citizenship in action (Gorard 2007a, 2007b). There is similarly a key role for the pupils. Having friends is important, and also avoidance of being mistreated by other pupils. Those reporting being hurt, bullied and having things stolen by other pupils at school are all less likely to support extra help for others. This is not a school mix effect (e.g., where those attending schools with low levels of theft are more supportive anyway). Thus, it appears to stem directly from treatment by others. Some of the differences are slight. For example, 44% of pupils who had been bullied were in support of help for others, compared to 51% who had not been bullied (or were not prepared to say). Nevertheless, there could also be a role for teachers here then, in preventing such mistreatment and educating the potential bullies and thieves.

Learning to trust at school?

How then do pupils learn to trust teachers to act fairly on their behalf? Only 44% of pupils agreed that their teachers were generally fair, therefore any prediction of who reported this would be 56% accurate just by assuming that no one did. Using this binary outcome in a regression model, we can explain a very high proportion (45%) of the remaining differences in responses. The majority of variation in responses is explicable by pupils' experiences at school (Table 10.3). There is a much smaller role for pupil background and parental relationship, and no school mix here at all. Young people in England are much more likely to agree that their teachers are fair (1.75 times as much) than pupils from the other countries. This is an even stronger indication of underlying

Table 10.3 Percentage of pupils correctly identified as trusting teachers or not, by batch of variables

Batch	Percentage predicted correctly	Percentage of remaining variation explained
Base figure	56	–
Pupil background	60	9
Aggregated background	60	0
Parental support	62	5
Experience of justice at school	78	36
Total	–	45

Table 10.4 Coefficients for pupil/school experience variables and whether trusting or not

Teachers punished bad behaviour fairly	1.72
Teachers treated my opinion with respect	1.67
Teachers have been interested in my well-being	1.67
Teachers treated all pupils' opinions with respect	1.67
My marks usually reflected the quality of my work	1.61
Teachers encouraged me to make my own mind up	1.45
My marks usually reflected the effort I made	1.43
Teachers continued explaining until all understood	1.32

Note: All coefficients in this table and the others like it are calculated in relation to the strongly disagree category. Not all variables are displayed.

good relationships between teachers and pupils in England than in the prior section. Those from families in which the father has a professional occupation are slightly more likely to agree that they trusted teachers (1.15 times). However, the combined influence of these background variables is considerably less than for willingness to help others (see above). Having parents interested in their well-being and who respect their opinions is also related to reported trust of teachers (both 1.67).

It is again the pupils' experiences at school that are the main determinants of trust here (Table 10.4). Positive results and relations with teachers are important factors related to whether pupils trust others – not perhaps very surprisingly. Teachers have to be seen to be following principles of equity properly by respecting all pupils, respecting individual pupil autonomy, and showing concern for all. They must also be prepared to reward and punish pupils when this is warranted, and to remember not to carry this discrimination over into areas of school life where it is not warranted. Pupils who had been bullied at school were also more likely to report trusting their teachers to be fair (not in the table). It is not clear whether this is because it was another pupil who was the bully and the teacher who helped or sorted it out, or if there is another explanation or none at all.

Learning whether school is fair?

Fractionally over 50% of pupils agree school is a fair place. Who are these pupils and how do they differ from the other 50%? As in the last example, it is the experiences at school that are key with a smaller role for background and parents (Table 10.5). Pupils in Italy are considerably more likely to agree that their school was fair than those in the other countries (2.08 times as likely, all other things being equal). This reflects the impression gained from Chapter 7 that in several respects pupils in Italy report the fewest injustices at school. And pupils with high marks (1.27), and those reporting that their parents talk to them about their friends, interests (both 1.85), and school (2.08) are more likely to find school fair.

The positive experiences linked to a fair school include the justifiably discriminatory ideas of justice – where differential marks and punishments are deserved and so fair (Table 10.6). They also include the universal ideas of justice – where respect and care are important for all without differentiation – and some unpleasant experiences with other pupils. The picture is very similar to that for learning to trust teachers.

Table 10.5 Percentage of pupils correctly identified as agreeing school was a fair place or not, by batch of variables

Batch	Percentage predicted correctly	Percentage of remaining variation explained
Base figure	50	–
Pupil background	56	12
Aggregated background	56	0
Parental support	59	6
Experience of justice at school	78	38
Total	–	56

Table 10.6   Coefficients for pupil/school experience variables and agreeing school was a fair place

Pupils got the marks they deserved	2.27
Teachers punished bad behaviour fairly	2.13
I have good friends in school	1.79
Teachers continued explaining until all understood	1.69
All pupils were treated the same way in class	1.61
Teachers have been interested in my well-being	1.47
Teachers treated pupils' opinions with respect	1.28
I enjoyed working with other pupils	1.13
Something of mine was stolen	0.80
I was bullied by other pupils	0.56

Note: All coefficients are in relation to the strongly disagree category.

We will see later how similar this set of potential determinants is to pupils learning about whether society is fair, and whether people can be trusted more generally. Negative experiences, such as bullying at the hands of pupils here, correspondingly reduce the perceived fairness of schools. This seems reasonable and could suggest that the result about bullying discussed in the last section is anomalous.

Predicting professional aspiration

We now move on to consider possible outcomes of school and family background that concern future life or wider society. Professional aspiration was used as the dependent variable in a binary logistic regression. In total, 48% of pupils reported wanting a professional occupation after leaving education, and the remaining 52% did not. Any prediction that an individual pupil had an aspiration to a professional occupation would be 52% correct simply assuming that no one wished to be a professional. The success of the model depends on its ability to improve on this baseline figure. The percentage predicted correctly for each stage of the model is in Table 10.7. As can be seen, the model is reasonably successful in predicting aspiration over and above the baseline figure, especially given the likely variation in occupational structure between countries, which cannot be picked up here. A further 21 percentage points (over and above 52%) are explicable in total, which is 44% of the outstanding 48% of variation otherwise unexplained. Of this increase, almost all is accounted for by pupil background characteristics, and school-level figures for pupil background (the school mix). Unusually for

Table 10.7   Percentage of pupils correctly identified as having professional aspiration or not, by batch of variables

Batch	Percentage predicted correctly	Percentage of remaining variation explained
Base figure	52	–
Pupil background	64	25
Aggregated background	71	15
Parental support	71	0
Experience of justice at school	73	4
Total	–	44

this study, only a small amount of the remaining variation is accounted for by pupils' reported experience of justice at school.

Of the pupil background factors, once other characteristics are taken into account, whether the pupil was born in the country of the survey or not, and whether their parents were born in the survey country, are not relevant to aspiration. This suggests fairness of a kind, in that those pupils born outside the country of the survey or with one or more parents born elsewhere have the same level of professional aspiration as 'indigenous' pupils (see also Chapter 8).

The most important predictor of aspiration is (self-reported) level of attainment at school – used as an indicator of academic talent. Pupils reporting high attainment are 2.39 times as likely as those reporting low attainment to want a professional occupation, *ceteris paribus*. Similarly, pupils reporting average attainment are 1.57 times as likely as low attainers to want a professional occupation. So, one interpretation is that low attaining pupils have lower occupational aspirations. Where we have been able to verify these self-reports of attainment with Key Stage results (for the England sample), they are reasonably accurate. However, it is also possible that both of these subjective variables are simply picking up the same level of confidence in self-reports.

If attainment is put aside for this reason, and so removed from the analysis, the most important influence on aspiration is, unsurprisingly, the occupation of parents. For example, 59% of pupils with professional fathers also want a professional career, compared to 45% for children of skilled workers, and 41% for children of those in unskilled or no employment. Pupils with professional mothers are 1.38 times as likely to report professional aspirations, as those with mothers having an unskilled job or no job. The figure (odds) for professional fathers is 1.58. It is unclear from this survey whether this is a kind of direct reproduction or whether there are latent forms of capital in professional families that lead to higher aspiration among children. Lesser influences are sex (females 1.09 times as likely as males), first language (those speaking home language 1.10 times as likely those speaking it as a second language), and father attending university (1.14 times as likely as those not having been to university). So aspiration is stratified by social and educational background in just the same way as attainment is regularly found to be (Gorard 2000b).

When the pupil background variables are aggregated to the school level, as an estimate of the school mix effect of clustering similar pupils in schools and classes, they can further improve the predictions of aspirations. One interpretation of this is that there is a school mix effect on pupil aspiration. So, for example, as well as the pupil's father's occupation being a good predictor (see above), the percentage of professional fathers in each school is also a good predictor. In fact, the odds of aspiring to a professional occupation increase 1.02 times for each percentage of the school intake with professional fathers. This is a very large increase in addition to the impact of the pupil's own father (since the odds here are multiplied by the relevant percentage of school intake). The mother's occupation is slightly less important (1.01), but where they were born is somewhat more important. The odds of aspiring to a professional occupation increase 1.03 times for each percentage of the school intake with mothers born in the survey country. Or put another way, while the country of origin of each pupil is not apparently relevant to their aspirations, having schools with high concentrations of pupils with mothers from another country reduces aspirations. Where the pupil and the father were born does not seem to matter so much once the origin of the mother is taken into account. The odds of aspiring to a professional occupation increase 1.01 times for each percentage of the school intake speaking the language of the survey country at home, regardless of the language spoken by an individual pupil.

Those attending a school with a high percentage of pupils from professional, educated families tend to have higher aspirations even where they are from different kinds of families themselves. If accepted, this finding has a clear message for the promotion of social justice via the school mix. Allowing pupils from professional, educated families to cluster in specific schools will encourage social reproduction. There is no gain in such clustering, since there is no clear school mix on attainment (Gorard 2006b, and see Chapter 2). There is a cost in terms of social mobility. Thus, as with many analyses, but this time in terms of social justice, we conclude that comprehensive and undifferentiated schools are the best as a system (Gorard 2007b).

The clustering of parents who have been to university is not relevant once these other factors are taken into account. More importantly from a policy perspective, the backwards stepwise regression also eliminated the percentage of boys and girls and the percentage of high, average and low attainment pupils as predictors. Thus, as far as we can tell from this survey, putting girls (and boys) in separate schools does not influence their aspiration once their background is factored in. Similarly, selecting pupils to school by (self-reported) attainment neither increases nor decreases their aspiration. It is socioeconomic segregation between schools that matters here.

The survey included four questions about the pupil's relationship with parents, and the kinds of interest and support their parents provided. Using these variables makes no difference to the quality of the prediction and all four items are eliminated in backward stepwise selection.

There is a small but discernible relationship, once the preceding factors are accounted for, between pupils' reports of justice in school and their aspirations. While background is very important and school structure (such as segregation) is important in producing aspiration, there is still a small role for the interaction of teachers and pupils at school.

In terms of policy, an interesting result is that whether a pupil repeats a year or more (i.e., born before 1991) makes no difference to aspiration (*ceteris paribus*). Pupils strongly agreeing that they get on well with teachers are much more likely to report wanting a professional occupation. Those strongly agreeing were 1.30 times as likely as those strongly disagreeing to want a professional occupation. If there is any causal link here it is unclear. It might be that some teachers play a role in reducing the hopes of some pupils (see Chapter 8). Pupils strongly agreeing that teachers respected their opinions were 1.25 times as likely, as those strongly disagreeing, to want a professional occupation. These two items both relate to the individual pupil and their relationship with teachers. Those pupils with professional aspiration tend to report better individual and personal relationships with teachers.

However, the opposite is true when we consider pupil–teacher relationships in general. Pupils with professional aspirations tend to identify the unfair treatment of others. Those strongly agreeing that teachers respected all pupils' opinions were less likely to have professional aspirations (0.88) than those strongly disagreeing. Similarly, those strongly agreeing that they trusted teachers to be fair had the lowest aspirations

(0.84). Otherwise, in general, those with the most positive personal experience of school had the highest aspirations (or *vice versa* of course). Those strongly agreeing that they had good friends at school were 1.72 times as likely to want a professional job. Those agreeing that they were discouraged easily, and that school was a waste of item, had the lowest aspirations. However, the model was also run with this last variable omitted on theoretical grounds. It could be interpreted as an outcome of schooling as well as an experience. Whether it was included or not made little difference to the other predictors.

Predicting levels of trust beyond school

Whether most people can be trusted was another outcome used as a dependent variable in a binary logistic regression. In total, 51% of pupils reported not trusting people generally, and the remaining 49% trusted people to some extent. Any prediction of an individual pupil trusting people could be 51% correct simply by assuming that no one trusted people. The success of the model depends on its ability to improve on this baseline figure. The percentage predicted correctly for each stage of the model is in Table 10.8. Pupil background characteristics explain some of the variation in outcomes but not as much as might be expected. And this influence mostly operates at the individual level, with no evidence of a school mix effect. Of the increase in our ability to make correct predictions over and above the baseline, nearly half is attributable to experiences of justice at school. This is after background and parental support have been taken into account, and so represents reasonable evidence of the influence of school, just as with learning to trust teachers (see Table 10.3 above).

Table 10.8 Percentage of pupils correctly identified as trusting people or not, by batch of variables

Batch	Percentage predicted correctly	Percentage of remaining variation explained
Base figure	51	–
Pupil background	56	10
Aggregated background	56	0
Parental support	57	2
Experience of justice at school	62	10
Total	–	22

Insofar as we can explain a tendency to trust people with these survey data, pupil background is a factor. The sex, language, and country of origin of the pupil are irrelevant to this issue of learning to trust most people. Also irrelevant are the occupations of parents and country of origin of mothers. Those with a father born in the survey country are slightly more trusting (1.08). Another determinant of this improvement in the baseline model lies in the (self-reported) attainment of pupils. Intriguingly, pupils reporting higher levels of attainment at school are somewhat less likely to report trust (0.94) than average attainers who are in turn less likely than low attainers (1.05). Whether this is due to greater perspicacity, or another confounding variable, is not clear.

The survey included four questions about the pupil's relationship with parents. Using these variables makes a small difference to the quality of the prediction. Parents talking to pupils about their friends and interests, and being interested in their well-being, are irrelevant here. Those whose parents treat them with respect and talk to them about school tend to be more trusting. Those who strongly agree that their parents treat them with respect have odds of 1.13 relative to those who strongly disagree. Those who strongly agree that their parents talk to them about school have relative odds of 1.12.

There is a very clear relationship, once the preceding factors are accounted for, between pupils' reports of justice in school and their sense of trust in other people. While background is important in producing trust, the biggest factor among the items surveyed is the reported interaction with teachers and pupils at school. Those who report getting along well with their teachers, and trusting their teachers to be fair, are more trusting in general. Of course, there is a possible element of tautology in several of these 'independent' variables. Unlike aspirations, whether a pupil repeats a year or more (i.e., born before 1991) makes a small negative difference to trust (0.93). Pupils who have repeated one or more years are less likely to be trusting (41%) than those who have not (50%), perhaps linked to the lack of grade repetition in England where teachers are deemed fairer. However, it is actual experiences at school that are most strongly related to trust. Pupils who regard school and teachers as fair, and the meting out of punishments as fair, and who have not been hurt or isolated by other pupils nor had something stolen are, perhaps understandably, more trusting. As with others outcomes, this suggests a clear role for teachers in educating citizens who are generally trusting of others. They do this through their exemplification of good (or indeed poor) citizenship in action. There is also a more direct role for teachers in preventing the mistreatment of some pupils by others and educating any potential 'bullies' or 'thieves' (Table 10.9).

Table 10.9   Coefficients for pupil/school experience variables and trusting people or not

School was fair	1.40
I enjoyed working with other pupils	1.27
Teachers punished fairly	1.23
Marks reflect quality	1.18
I trusted my teachers to be fair	1.17
I have a friend who gets low marks	1.14
All pupils were treated the same	1.10
Something of mine was stolen	0.89
I felt invisible to my friends	0.86
Teacher got angry with me in front of the class	0.86
I got discouraged easily	0.82

Avoidance of bullying, personal violence, and theft are related to learning to trust others – or put the other way, the least trusting are those who have been victims of bullying, violence, and theft at school. Therefore, there is an argument that what happens at school differentially influences pupils' sense of what is just and fair, and what wider society is like. And a lot of what happens is the direct responsibility of other pupils, while only indirectly due to the (in)actions of teachers. If citizenship education entails learning appropriate levels of trust in others, then the level of reported mistreating of pupils by other pupils is a clear barrier to progress.

Learning about the use of violence?

We can explain very little of the variation between pupils prepared to hit others and those not prepared to hit, except via their experiences at school (Table 10.10). Partly this is because, thankfully, the responses are skewed towards disagreement, with only 32% of pupils ageing with violence in this way. Nevertheless, there is a marked tendency towards agreement in the Czech Republic (odds of 2.00 compared to the other countries), which could be a consequence of the exact strength of meaning of the question in translation. If not, this is an alarming finding. Those pupils speaking the language of the survey country (0.79), or who had fathers born in that country (0.83), were slightly less likely than others to agree with this proposition. Pupils reporting parents who talk to them about school (0.56) and who are interested in their well-being (0.57) are also considerably less likely to agree with hurting others.

Table 10.10 Percentage of pupils correctly identified as agreeing it is OK to hit others or not, by batch of variables

Batch	Percentage predicted correctly	Percentage of remaining variation explained
Base figure	68	–
Pupil background	69	3
Aggregated background	69	0
Parental support	70	3
Experience of justice at school	77	22
Total	–	28

Table 10.11 Coefficients for pupil/school experience variables and agreeing it is OK to hit others

School has been a waste of time for me	3.33
Teachers had favourite pupils	1.41
Teachers continued explaining until all understood	1.32
Hard-working pupils were usually treated the best	1.25
I feel as though I am invisible to my school mates	0.81

The experiences most associated with pupils agreeing to the acceptability of violence are a strange set (Table 10.11). The strongest association is with school being a waste of time, but if there is a causal model here it is unclear. It is also not clear why teachers explaining until all understood might be linked in this way. Perhaps it is a spurious association of the kind that any analysis of this size is likely to throw up – especially as the baseline figure is so skewed. Again, however, the experience of teachers apparently misusing principles of justice in the wrong contexts leads to negative outcomes. Having favourites such as hard-working pupils and treating them better even in contexts where effort is not relevant, such as respect and autonomy, could lead some susceptible pupils also to misapprehend otherwise widespread criteria of equity.

Integration or multiculturalism?

A slight majority of pupils agree that people moving to their country should adopt local customs. This means that any attempt to predict

Table 10.12 Percentage of pupils correctly identified as agreeing that immigrants should adopt local customs or not, by batch of variables

Batch	Percentage predicted correctly	Percentage of remaining variation explained
Base figure	54	–
Pupil background	59	11
Aggregated background	60	2
Parental support	60	0
Experience of justice at school	70	22
Total	–	35

which pupils agree would be 54% successful simply by assuming that all agree. Our model improves that figure by now explaining 35% of the previously unexplained variation in responses (Table 10.12). It suggests a role for both pupil background and experience of school. Pupils in the Czech Republic, where there are far fewer recent immigrants, are considerably more likely to agree that immigrants should adapt to the customs of their new home (1.43) than pupils in other countries. This difference could be due to a lack of experience of immigrants in the Czech Republic among all pupils, or it could be due to a lack of the immigrants themselves who might otherwise disagree with the idea and prefer a form of multiculturalism. The latter interpretation is supported by the fact that pupils with fathers (1.49) and mothers (1.19) born in the country of the survey were more likely to agree with the integration idea. Pupils born in the survey country (1.20) and speaking the language of that country (1.23) were also more likely to agree. Pupils with recent immigrant experience were overall far less likely to agree to everyone adopting the customs of their new country. However, the Czech result could also be partly about lack of actual experience of immigration (ignorance) because there is also a school mix result here. Pupils in schools with lower levels of recent immigrants (as assessed by the same variables, like where they or their parents were born) were somewhat more likely to agree with immigrant adoption of local customs. Note that this is additional to, and after the model has catered for, whether they themselves are recent immigrants. It is young people who are not immigrants themselves but who are in schools with higher levels of recent immigrants who are slightly more in favour of a multicultural approach. This is an important finding for the school mix.

Table 10.13 Coefficients for pupil/school experience variables and agreeing that immigrants should adopt local customs

I have good friends in school	1.67
I have a friend who gets low marks at school	1.32
Hard-working pupils were usually treated best	1.15
Teachers treated my opinion with respect	0.81
I have a friend who does not come from [country of survey]	0.68

Turning to the school experience results, perhaps because recent immigrants are less likely to report having good friends at school, and because they are less in favour of adopting local customs, these two ideas are strongly linked (Table 10.13). Similarly, recent immigrants are more likely to have friends born elsewhere. Low attainers at school are both more likely to have a friend who is also a low attainer and to want immigrants to fit in. But again, teachers apparently misusing a principle of justice and treating hard-working pupils better even where it is not relevant, and not respecting the opinions of pupils, are linked to what could be construed as a long-term negative outcome of schooling.

Summary

It is difficult to do justice to the scale and variety of evidence presented in Chapters 7–9, and now partly combined in this chapter. There is some excellent news for equity in schools and society. In many respects, pupil background, their family, and the type of school they attend (or even for those who do not attend school) are all unrelated to their experiences of justice and injustice. Equity in schools and other educational institutions is considerably less stratified than attainment is. The situation is not ideal, because there clearly are still injustices occurring. But the fact that these experiences are not especially stratified should make them easier to address, in distinction to the stubborn inequalities in attainment that developed countries have tried to reduce over decades.

Having supportive parents helps a little (on these admittedly rather restricted measures of parental support). Pupil and family background is important to professional aspiration and to learning to trust most people, but less important for all other outcomes discussed here. There are few robust international differences, that survive multivariate analysis to assess whether they are really country specific, or to do with different sub-samples (or even school populations) in the different countries. Pupils in England, *ceteris paribus*, are more likely to agree to help for others, and more likely to trust their teachers. Pupils in the Czech Republic are more likely to condone hitting another pupil or lying to evade punishment. Pupils in Italy are more likely to report that their school was fair. The school mix or pattern of peers in school is important for aspiration and views on the inclusion of recent immigrants, and this mix acts over and above the influence of individual pupil background.

However, the bulk of variation in responses that we can explain is linked to pupils' experiences at school. This is true whether the outcome of interest relates to school – like learning to trust teachers – or it relates to wider society – like learning to trust most people. Willingness to help others, trusting people at school and more widely, finding school a fair place, not being prepared to hit another, and not insisting that immigrants must conform to local ways of life, could all be seen as thoughtful, tolerant and somewhat desirable outcomes of education. There is a small impact of attainment and from grade repetition on some of these outcomes, but other than these there are four themes that occur again and again. Positive outcomes for pupils are ameliorated by appropriate teacher respect for all pupils and their opinions, by teachers allowing pupils the autonomy to work at their own speed, by teachers using discrimination only in its proper domains (such as when marking pupil work), and by the lack of suffering at the hands of other pupils. Whatever is intended to be taught formally within them, schools as societies are educational in themselves. What are the implications?

11
The Practical Implications of Reconsidering What Schools Are For

In this final chapter we first discuss briefly the nature of the research we undertook. We do this to try and ensure for ourselves, and to assure others, that the implications we are drawing from it are warranted. Then, we summarise the key findings from the book in terms of their practical implications for nations, school systems, educational leaders, teachers, and families.

The research

We have, as is our research custom, added caveats about our study and findings throughout the book, and we summarise some of them again here.

It is important to recall that a lot of potentially important things remain unmeasured in our survey of pupils. The school-level characteristics, for example, have mostly had to be estimated by simply aggregating the responses of those pupils who respond. In addition, we cannot claim that the samples are perfectly representative, nor the questions perfectly phrased for each language, despite back-translation. There is inevitably some non-response, both at school and pupil level. Other deficiencies of the dataset include the lack of background information on the Japanese pupils, and some miscoding of country of origin for pupils' mothers in England. More importantly, in our analysis we are associating some parts of the reports of pupils with other parts of the same reports. There is no definitive test of a causal model here, and even a danger of elements of tautology in some of the associations reported. We have no prior evidence of the sense of justice of pupils, of the kind that could be used to assess the progress made over a period of time at school. Regression techniques are anyway infamous for dredging datasets and finding spurious patterns *post hoc* (Gorard 2006c).

As a research team, we set out to use some of the individual pupil survey items, in combination, to construct indices or composite indicators of justice (of the kind that is routinely used in large surveys such as PISA). We had a theoretical framework for these, based upon our extensive and prolonged pilot work (see EGREES 2008), and some items were included precisely because they would form part of these constructs. However, our analysis was unable to confirm these constructs, and unable to create a coherent, parsimonious alternative to them. In fact, partly as a consequence of discussions within the team and partly because of the prior experience of the team from England, we now have serious doubts about all such attempts to create construct variables (see Gorard 2009b).

In summary, these are the kinds of problems that would occur in any real-life research project of this scale and ambition. Being aware of them, and making readers aware of them, is part of our defence to being misled by them.

Where there is overlap with prior projects between the questions asked and the methods used, our findings here replicate our earlier findings from our international 'quick survey' of 6000 pupils in Belgium, England, France, Italy, and Spain (EGREES 2005), our 2000 case pilot for the work described in this book (EGREES 2008), and our survey of 5000 students in England for the Qualifications and Curriculum Authority (see Gorard et al. 2009a, and Chapters 2 and 3). So we now have a body of evidence on some of these issues that covers nearly 20,000 pupils in seven countries worldwide. In addition, our survey results (self-reports of student attainment, for example) are in agreement with official and other data sources where a comparison is possible. The pupil comments whether given in conversation, focus groups, or written on the questionnaire, agree with and help us understand the survey results. Our presence in classrooms during delivery of the pilot survey, and the wonderful conversations that ensued, have assured us that the vast majority of pupils take the chance to express their views very seriously indeed.

Our efforts to avoid being misled by regression include using only robust and sizeable results, and trying a range of alternative models solely for the purpose of testing the volatility of the solutions we present in Chapter 10. There are no issues of significance (and so vanishing breakthroughs) here. We focus only on effect sizes (perhaps 5% or more of outstanding variance explained, and odds outside the range

0.8 and 1.2, for example) or on slightly smaller odds (such as 0.9 or 1.15 for categorical variables) that are consistent in scale and direction across different outcomes or groups of pupils. We entered potential explanatory variables in a theoretically coherent order to prevent unwanted proxies from dominating the analyses, but we also ran the models in reverse order to see if the substantive findings would change. The substantive findings did not change for the models we present in Chapter 10. We also compared each model to a precise equivalent derived from the same dataset and predictors, but with the outcome variable replaced by a random number with the same distribution over two categories (such as trusting teachers or not). These random models barely improved from the baseline figures, and this assured us that our published results are not spurious patterns. We also wanted to check the school mix results, where the pupil background variables aggregated to school level explain variance which is additional to that explained by the same variables at an individual level. Was the 'school mix' result merely an outcome of misspecification, such that the true impact of individual background was being obscured? Aggregating the variables for each stage in the model (such as relationship with parents) to school level yielded no improvement in predictions. Even aggregating the individual experiences at school to school level (such as finding the percentage of pupils who had been bullied in each school) when combined yielded only a fraction of 1% improvement in prediction for all models. Thus, the school mix result for pupil origin looks different, genuine, and useful.

The scale of relationship between the predictors such as pupil background, school mix or pupil experience of justice, and the outcome variables trialled here is substantial, over a large sample. The results are credible. Another way of imagining these findings is to compare them with the long-standing tradition of work on academic school effectiveness. School effectiveness, as a field, has the same problems as the work described here. It is not a causal test, does not have complete information, has to deal with omitted variables and missing cases, and so on. But our models are based on biography (and so the time sequence necessary for causation), rather than the nesting hierarchies or levels used in school effectiveness which perforce leave aside characteristics that do not nest, such as sex or parental support. Although our measures, of intrinsically hard to measure ideas in education, will be imprecise, they do not suffer from the problem of propagation of errors, as described for school effectiveness calculations in Chapter 2. In these respects, our findings are considerably more powerful than the school effects purportedly found in school effectiveness work. Thus, the findings are genuinely worth thinking about the consequences of.

It is time for us to drop the caveats. Government policy in education worldwide is routinely based on evidence from erroneous analyses, much smaller studies, or studies that make no attempt to provide a warrant for their conclusions. See, for example, the high impact study for England discussed in Gorard (2008e), in which major national policy affecting the social mobility of 60 million people is being based on around seven out of 17,000 adults appearing in an unexpected cell for a cross-tabulation, and on an error caused by using the wrong year in an international comparison. Billions of pounds are spent, at huge opportunity cost, on policies and practices that have no success, and no hope of success (such as the teacher effectiveness programme envisaged by Barber and Moursched 2007, see Chapter 2). Our work here is, we believe, recognisably different from these, and ready to be engineered into more useable forms for policy and practice. We make a start to that engineering process in the remaining sections of this chapter.

Implications for attainment, equity, and the school mix

In many ways, and as so often, some major findings of this study seem obvious and even incontrovertible in retrospect. Young people are influenced by their life at school, and learn to trust others partly as a consequence of how trustworthy others have appeared to be so far in their lives, for example. The reason our findings may be more contentious as a corpus than they are in isolation is that their implications for policy and practice run counter to so much of what is currently going on in education in policy terms. This is true for the developed countries that took part in our study, and in many of those that did not, including the United States.

First, and perhaps most radically, there is our conclusion from Chapter 2. Within a national school system in a welfare state it makes no discernible difference to a pupil's terminal qualifications which school that pupil attends. This means that a whole industry of school effectiveness and improvement in the United Kingdom (and presumably, in the United States, the Netherlands, and elsewhere) needs to adapt. We may have arrived at a near ideal situation of equity in academic provision in England with all of the differences, which are scientifically explicable, explained solely in terms of pupil intake. If so, there may not be a general awareness that we have reached this ideal because we are wedded to a zero-sum method of assessment that insists on winners and losers. So, how would we know if we had reached or neared that ideal? Improving the situation in one way must, because of the system used, lead to an apparent dis-improvement somewhere else. There are fixed degrees of freedom. So the situation is similar to the way that a medical advance like a vaccine for smallpox automatically condemns more people to deaths from heart attack or cancer. Successive administrations have made education a spending priority but have been perplexed that inequalities in attainment survive, and sometimes even grow as a result. Schools, by themselves, are simply not very good engines for overcoming the inequalities manifest in their pupil bodies, and it is wrong to expect them to do so quickly in one generation when exactly the same stubborn inequalities appear in other major areas of public policy as well – such as health, housing, and crime (Gorard et al. 2004).

Of course, in a system with much higher levels of tracking pupils than we find in England, streaming young people into different kinds of schools with very different possible futures, it may be that we would find bigger apparent differences between schools or types of schools. But this would not be a school effect. It would be a consequence of the different trajectories embarked on by young people in a system that selects, or at least bounds, their futures at the age of 7 or 11 (see Chapter 6). This is inherently unjust, and probably wasteful of talent as well. It is unjust because the earlier children are tracked like this the more likely it is that they will be inadvertently selected for tracks in terms of their background rather than their revealed talent. Anyway, in reality it would be almost impossible to test the differential effectiveness of tracks that led to clearly different outcomes (perhaps in terms of different qualifications, such as vocational or academic).

Tracking, selection by ability or aptitude, diversification of schools by mission, curriculum speciality, governance, or faith are all examples of attempts by governments to solve the unsolvable, and create a system consisting only of winners. But all of these initiatives are inimical to equity. In fact, what all of these initiatives have in common is that they tend to segregate the intakes to schools even more than would occur by chance, or by providing very similar schools but open to parental choice, or even through the dangerously simple procedure of allocating pupils to schools by area of residence (Gorard et al. 2003, Gorard 2009c).

In order to try and attain greater equality of outcome from schools, in terms of qualifications, the U.K. government and others (see Chapter 3) are increasingly turning to amending the qualifications themselves. While retaining apparent equality of treatment and of opportunity, new qualifications and modes of assessing them are devised, such as a series of vocational and technical initiatives in England, culminating at time of writing in the new National Diplomas (Gorard et al. 2009a). Given parity of esteem these vocational courses are meant to allow easy mixing of academic and vocational work-based routes from the age of 14. They may indeed do so, but recent history suggests that their take-up will be differential, and this will influence both the esteem in which the qualifications are held by others and encourage socioeconomic segregation of some kind between the routes. Something like the Diplomas could have been introduced nationwide, replacing all that had gone before. This may or may not have been a good idea, but it would at least have prevented what could turn out to be tracking (or at least tracking within institutions) by another name. One inequality, now based on the structure of institutions and the curricula they offer to different groups of pupils, could replace another, originally based on unequal outcomes in the same public examinations by identifiable social groups.

In England, the leaving age for compulsory education and training has been raised successively. School days get longer, holidays get shorter, initiatives like summer schools take place in the holidays. Children go to formal educational institutions with early-years provision increasingly early. There are more inspections and there is more regulation. There is more pressure on staff and more stress for the parents and pupils. And the reason for many of these changes is both to try and overcome inequalities in qualifications, and to raise the overall level of agreed skills even higher in order to be competitive in the international horse races represented by PISA, PIRLS or TIMSS (Huang 2009). The use of school improvement models has led, indirectly, to an overemphasis on the most visible indicators of schooling – examination and test scores. This marginalises other purposes and potential benefits of schooling. It suggests that *variations* in the scores themselves are largely the product of school effects when the evidence clearly shows otherwise. And it neglects the fact that the scores themselves are artificial, and technically difficult to compare fairly over subject, mode of assessment, level, time, or place (Gorard 2000b).

The evidence in this book points to another way. The clustering of pupils with similar backgrounds in their own schools, of the kind which is engendered by tracking, curriculum specialisation and the other attainment-driven initiatives described above, has no discernible influence on pupil attainment (Haahr et al. 2005, Horn 2009). But it *does* have an effect on something else. It reduces the potential role models for more disadvantaged pupils. As we have demonstrated in this book, clustering pupils with similar backgrounds in schools tends to strengthen social reproduction over generations. By depressing future aspiration, the clustering of similar pupils within schools is also related to their views on the integration of recent immigrants, and to a lesser extent it is related to learning to trust others. There is enough evidence from this and other studies to suggest that socially segregated school systems can endanger pupils' attitudes to schools and sense of belonging. This may be particularly pertinent in an era when purportedly disaffected and alienated (ethnic minority) youth are presented as a threat to social cohesion within and across communities in many European countries. Pupils in more socially segregated school systems simply report experiencing more unfairness.

Socially segregated systems are unfair to the most disadvantaged pupils, in comparison to comprehensive systems. Comprehensive systems of schools based on parental preference rather than selection or geographical criteria tend to produce narrower social differences in intake and outcomes (Hirsch 2002). Most available evidence therefore suggests that pupils with differing characteristics should be mixed in schools, rather than clustered by ability, sex, faith, finance, or country of origin. It seems that fairness for individuals, a sense of justice, and social cohesion and belonging are as much a product of experiences in schools, as lived in, as they are of the formal educational process. The mix of pupils in a school therefore matters more for social cohesion than school improvement (Gorard et al. 2003). This could affect patterns of post-compulsory participation and attainment as well. School experience combines with social background to form a relatively permanent lifelong learner or non-learner identity (Gorard and Selwyn 2005). What is true for aspirations appears also to be true for post-compulsory participation in education or training. Subsequent participation is influenced by the school mix (Gorard and Smith 2007).

To raise the occupational and educational aspirations of the most disadvantaged in society, a mixed school intake is desirable. Doing this is just, and is also likely to have economic returns for society (Levin 2009). One simple lever under our control is the policy of allocating pupils to schools. A mixed, comprehensive, and undifferentiated system of schools is preferable in this regard to a tracked, selective, faith-based or specialist one. The implications for policy are obvious. No selection, no faith-based schools, no curricular specialist schools for the core years, no division between schools responsible for their own admissions and the rest, no amount of private investment should allow maverick individuals control of state-funded schools, and so on. In fact, these are almost precisely the opposite of the policies of the government in the United Kingdom, and in many other countries.

Finally, for this section, it is worth observing that what is true between schools also applies within schools (see Chapter 3). Pupil aspiration, confidence, awareness of future opportunities, and preparedness for life beyond school are all enhanced through contact with pupils on other programmes of study, or in work-based settings. A consequence of acting on the desirability of all-ability comprehensive intakes to schools might be an increase in *within*-school setting and tracking. Also, where young people with very severe learning challenges are integrated into mainstream schools they will inevitably have some extra help and facilities. Our evidence is silent on the usefulness and dangers of such changes for academic outcomes, but for equity outcomes it is clear that these tracks within schools must not be mini-schools in themselves. Internal, perhaps vertical, divisions can be created within schools, and cross-age tutoring arranged, along with other activities that encourage pupils from different backgrounds and of different talents to mix, work, and play together. There will, perhaps inevitably, always be some young people who must remain educated apart, in institutions such as hospitals or secure units. The good news is that, in the two European countries reported on in Chapter 9, these young people feel at least as well cared for as the majority of pupils in mainstream schools.

Implications for equity and the preparation of teachers

Turning from what are largely national and regional policy issues, what do our findings say about teachers and their relationships with young people?

First, it is important to repeat that there is a high level of equity in all schools in all countries and as reported by all sub-groups of pupils. Many pupils enjoy their education, having been treated well at school, and feel that their learning has purpose. Most have good friends, and only a minority report unpleasant episodes such as bullying. Many pupils trust their teachers and find them helpful and supportive. These experiences show very little patterning in terms of the kinds of pupil background variables so often found to influence attainment. In most respects, pupil background, their family, and the type of school or institution they attend are only weakly related to their experiences of justice and injustice, if at all. The reports from pupils in high and low attaining, high and low poverty, and selective and comprehensive schools do not differ substantially. Those outside mainstream schooling were in many ways the most positive about their treatment and experiences. They often felt respected and cared for in appropriate ways. Recent immigrants generally report being well treated, and are at least as likely as others to have good relationships with teachers, and high hopes for the future. This is highly encouraging, since even if we were to conclude that some pupils are objectively disadvantaged, the pupils themselves are not aware of this or are not treated in an inferior way. Giving pupils a voice in research does not lead to a 'whingefest' in which pupils complain disproportionately about schools, teachers, and other pupils. Given that so much is working well and under control, at least according to the pupils who ought to be in a good position to judge, we are confident that the slightly more sophisticated issues of equity in education discussed below can now be dealt with effectively by the education systems of most developed countries.

Second, the fact that the differences in school experiences reported by pupils are not especially stratified should make them easier to address, in contrast to the inequalities in attainment that developed countries have tried to reduce over decades. The situation is not ideal, because there clearly are still injustices occurring. And, of course, it is hardly likely that everyone will ever be completely satisfied with their treatment. But the more widespread and repeated issues we identify can be addressed, quite easily, and for very little resource. This can be done mostly through reminding developing teachers of the underlying principles of justice and the domains within which learners see them as applicable.

Third, while the link between pupil background and most school experiences is weak, the link between school experiences and pupils' views on justice at school and beyond is strong. It is also repeated across many aspects of our results. We propose that school experiences are therefore assumed to be part of a causal determining sequence in the creation or entrenchment of pupils' views on what a fair world would be like and whether a fair world is possible. Interactional justice at school has long-term beneficial impacts.

It is quite clear that pupils' willingness to help others, their trust in people both at school and more widely, their experience of school as fair, and their views on violence and the integration of recent immigrants, among others, are all influenced by their experiences of schooling. Insofar as we are able to prefer one of the outcomes in any of these areas (such as that pupils express a willingness to help others, rather than not help), then the more 'positive' outcomes are mostly encouraged by:

- appropriate teacher respect for all pupils and their opinions
- teachers allowing pupils the autonomy to work at their own speed
- teachers using discrimination only in its proper domains
- and lack of abuse at the hands of other pupils

We deal briefly with each of these themes in turn.

Respect

Equity is difficult to define, but for us it represents that sense of fairness which underlies decisions about the principles of justice to apply in different domains for a given set of actors. Put simply, it is an internal template forming part of how we know something is fair. In specific situations there is considerable agreement, among pupils, about what is fair and what is unfair. Equity is an important ideal for education, in terms of school as a lived experience as well as its longer-term outcomes for citizens and society. Where equity is denied, negative consequences follow.

An example of equity in classroom interactions is represented by teachers' respect for their pupils' opinions, even when they might disagree with the pupils. Disagreement is an important part of learning. Encouraging the ideas, arguments, and evidence advanced by pupils, on the other hand, encourages learning. Respect for the individual despite a difference of opinion, and even where the pupil ideas are demonstrably incorrect or facile to the more sophisticated teacher, encourages a sense of personal autonomy and self-worth in the young person. It, therefore, influences the pupil's self-perceived position in social interactions, particularly vis-à-vis figures of authority. There is widespread agreement among all young people that all pupils should be treated with respect by teachers, their opinions should be valued, and that they should not be humiliated in any way. Few report that this takes place consistently, however. There is, therefore, a clear mismatch between what pupils want and what they experience, in many ways. This needs to be addressed urgently.

Autonomy

A very similar mismatch appears in the findings for pupil autonomy. It was clear from all forms of evidence that control of the pace of their own learning was important to nearly all young people. Both in comments about classroom processes and in their responses to questions about teachers' explanation, pupils made it clear that this very simple personalisation of their learning is too often missing.

The term 'equity' appears in the curriculum and some professional development resources used in initial teacher education in England and elsewhere. But the conception of equity used within them is often very limited – confined to the boy/girl attainment gap in one example. We propose that the apparently conflicting principles of justice, developed from something like Table 5.1, should be part of the development of all teachers, in all developed countries like those taking part in this study. It would help emerging teachers to distinguish between the universal principles (i.e., applicable to all participants in the setting), such as autonomy and respect, and the principles that legitimately require discrimination.

Discrimination

An important finding to emerge from this work, and one which has implications for implementing an effective curriculum for citizenship in schools, is that teachers were not always perceived to be treating pupils fairly and consistently. A common view was that teachers had pupils who were their favourites, that rewards and punishments were not always applied fairly, and that certain groups of pupils were treated less fairly than others. How can a curriculum for citizenship, which embraces issues of fairness and democracy, be effectively implemented if the pupils themselves do not mostly believe that their teachers are generally capable of fairness and support for democracy in school? In one sense, it does not really matter what the curriculum states about citizenship compared to the importance for pupils of experiencing mixed ethnic, sex and religious groups in non-racist and non-sexist settings, and genuine participation in the decision making of the schools.

Pupils want marks to reflect the quality of their work, or the effort they put in. Where necessary, they want punishments to be meted out consistently. Too many pupils report that this does not happen. Pupils do not want hard-working pupils to be favoured (except in assessment terms). Most report that this does not happen. Pupils are happy for their assessed work to be discriminated in terms of quality and effort, but they complain that hard-working, high-attaining pupils should not otherwise be favoured by teachers. This is a clear and strict application of the principle of merit, and one which teachers are widely misusing, by using it in the wrong settings.

We recommend, again as part of teacher continuing development, that teachers be prepared to keep a continuous watch on their apparent tendency to stray into domains inappropriate to the principles of fairness they are using. Pupils are not especially naïve. They know that teachers will get along better with some young people than others, and that they may even have favourites. All relationships are like that, and are not inequitable in themselves. But being more friendly with one pupil than another is very different from showing more respect to one of them or punishing another more severely for the same offence. Again, it is the transfer of differential treatment to another setting (another column in Table 5.1) that makes it unfair. It is the combination of actors, settings, and principles that help decide what is fair treatment.

Abuse

Those pupils treated best at school tend to have the most positive outlook on trust, civic values, and sense of justice. And *vice versa*. The worst reported incidents at school, both in pupil discussions and in the survey itself, came from the actions of other pupils in the form of social isolation, bullying, stealing, and violence. As our evidence shows, teachers still have two ways in which they can take responsibility for these actions by other pupils. First, and most obviously, teachers must stamp these incidents out wherever they are encountered. Perhaps more significantly for the readers of this book so far, teachers have a more general role in helping families and others in inhibiting such negative cycles of behaviour. Pupils who are prepared to condone lying and hitting another pupil are themselves influenced, at least to a small extent, by their experiences of justice in school. This cycles us back to the importance of the school mix, because abuses like classroom bullying might be made worse by socially segregated settings (Sreekanth 2009).

Conclusion

Fairness for individuals, a sense of justice, and social cohesion are as much a product of experiences in schools, as lived in, as they are of the formal educational process. Social, ethnic, and economic segregation matters, but not primarily for the sake of test results. It does not make sense to have a society preaching racial tolerance within a racially segregated school system, for example. For pupils their schools are their life, and not merely a preparation for it. Equitable treatment in schools matters for today, for the range of experiences of each pupil, for social cohesion, and to allow schools to teach important aspects of citizenship without being open to the charge of being hypocritical. Citizenship is about developing social and moral responsibility, and 'entails treating young people with respect and giving them meaningful fora in which their views can be aired' (Kerr 2003, p. 28). In order to educate for democracy, schools have to be more democratic than they have been traditionally. It is not enough that legislation gives rights to pupils. They have a right to know their rights and be encouraged to use them (Dobozy 2007).

In conclusion, our message is that schools and teachers may want to concern themselves a little less with the efficiency and effectiveness of their approach to instruction, and a little more with the kind of people they want their charges to be. If they do, they should listen to the criteria of justice revealed here by the voices of pupils from England to Japan, and learn for themselves that, in some respects at least, pupils know more than their teachers. Pupils have quite clear views on what is fair, and are generally willing and able to express those views, given a chance. They appear to be responsible commentators on a process of education that they are intimately involved in. Are research users willing to acknowledge and act on those views? By denying some pupils justice at school, whether inadvertently or not by our overemphasis on the importance of pedagogy, we are in danger of prolonging and exacerbating injustice in society. Schools, in their structure and organisation, can do more than simply reflect the society we have; they can try to be the precursor of the kind of society that we wish to have.

Appendix

We present here the full formula mentioned in Chapter 2, and used by DCSF in England to calculate CVA scores. The Key Stage 4 (KS4) prediction for any pupil in 2007 was given as:

162.1
+0.3807 * (the squared school average KS2 score)
−5.944 * (school average KS2 score)
+1.396 * (KS2 English points − school average KS2 score)
−0.109 * (KS2 maths points − school average KS2 score)
−27.1 (if in care)
−59.51 * (IDACI score)
−34.37 (if School Action SEN)
−65.76 (if Action Plus or statement of SEN)
−73.55 (if joined after September of year 10)
−23.43 (if joined not in July/August/September of years 7–9)
+14.52 (if female)
−12.94 * (age within year, where 31 August is 0 and 1 September is 1)
+ *for English as an additional language pupils only* (−8.328 −0.1428 * (school average KS2 score)^2 + 4.93 * school average KS2 score)
+ ethnicity coefficient, from a pre-defined table (such as 0 for White and 29.190 for Black African pupils)
+ *for FSM pupils only* (−22.9 + FSM/ethnicity interaction, from a pre-defined table)
+ 1.962 * (cohort average KS2 score)
− 4.815 * (standard deviation of cohort average KS2 score)

References

Amrein-Beardsley, A. (2008) Methodological concerns about the education value-added assessment system, *Educational Researcher*, 37, 2, 65–75.

Bald, J. (2006) Inspection is now just a numbers game, *Times Educational Supplement*, 26 May, 21.

Barber, M. and Moursched, M. (2007) *How the World's Best-Performing School Systems Come Out on Top*, London: McKinsey & Co.

Baye, A. (2005) Entre efficacité et équité: ce que les indicateurs de l'OECD veulent dire, in Demeuse, M., Baye, A., Straeten, M., Nicaise, J., and Matoul, A. (eds), *Vers une école juste et efficace, 26 contributions sur les systèmes d'enseignement et de formation*, Coll. Economie, Société, Région, De Boeck, Bruxelles, 539–558.

Baye, A., Demeuse, M., Monseur, C. and Goffin, C. (2006) *A Set of Indicators to Measure Equity in 25 European Union Education Systems*, Report submitted to the European Commission, Directorate General Education and Culture, Bruxelles.

Boudon, R. (1973) *Education, Opportunity and Social Inequality*, New York: Praeger.

Boudon, R. (1995) A propos des sentiments de justice: nouvelles remarques sur la Théorie de Rawls, *L'Année Sociologique*, 45, 2, 273–95.

Boulton, M., Duke. E., Holma, G., Laxton, E., Nicholas, B., Spells, R., Williams, E. and Woodmansey, H. (2009) Associations between being bullied, perceptions of safety in classroom and playground, and relationship with teacher among primary school pupils, *Educational Studies*, 35, 3, 255–267.

Burgess, S., Wilson, D. and Lupton, R. (2005) Parallel lives? Ethnic segregation in schools and neighbourhoods, *Urban Studies*, 42, 7, 1027–1056.

Casey, L., Davies, P., Kalambouka, A., Nelson, N. and Boyle, B. (2006) The influence of schooling on the aspirations of young people with special educational needs, *British Educational Research Journal*, 32, 2, 273–290.

Christensen, P. (2004) The health-promoting family: A conceptual framework for future research Social Science and Medicine, *Social Science And Medicine*, 59, 377–387.

Civic Education Study (2001) *IEA Civic Education Study*, http://www2.hu-berlin.de/empir_bf/iea_e.html, accessed January 2005.

Clotfelter, C. (2001) Are whites still fleeing? Racial patterns and enrolment sifts in urban public schools, *Journal of Policy Analysis and Management*, 20, 2, 199–221.

Coleman, J., Campbell, E., Hobson, C., McPartland, J., Mood, A., Weinfield, F. and York, R. (1966) *Equality of Educational Opportunity*, Washington, D.C.: U.S. Government Printing Office.

Coleman, J., Hoffer, T. and Kilgore, S. (1982) Cognitive outcomes in public and private schools, *Sociology of Education*, 55, 2/3, 65–76.

Cowell, K., Howe, B. and McNeil, J. (2008) 'If there's a dead rat, don't leave it'. Young children's understanding of their citizenship rights and responsibilities, *Cambridge Journal of Education*, 38, 3, 321–339.

Davie, R. and Galloway, D. (1996) The voice of children in education, in R.Davie and D. Galloway (eds), *Listening to Children in Education.* London: David Fulton.

Davies, I. and Evans, M. (2002) Encouraging active citizenship, *Educational Review*, 54, 1, 69–78.

Davies, I., Gorard, S. and McGuinn, N. (2005) Citizenship studies and character studies: Similarities and contrasts, *British Journal of Educational Studies*, 53, 3, 341–358.

DCSF (2007) *A Technical Guide to the Contextual Value Added 2007 Model*, http://www.dcsf.gov.uk/performancetables/primary_07/2007GuidetoCVA.pdf, accessed 16 December 2008.

De Schauwer, E., Van Hove, G., Mortier, K. and Loots, G. (2009) I need help on Mondays; it's not my day; the other days, I'm OK: Perspectives of disabled children on inclusive education, *Children and Society*, 23, 99–111.

DeCocker, G. (2002) What do National Standards really mean? in DeCocker, G. (ed). *National Standards and School Reform in Japan and the US*. New York: Teachers College Press.

Demeuse, M. (2004) A set of equity indicators of the European Systems: A synthesis, in L. Moreno Herrera and G. Francia (eds), *Educational Policies: Implications for Equity, Equality and Equivalence*, Reports from the Department of Education. Orebro (Sweden): Orebro University.

Demeuse, M., Derobertmasure, A., Friant, N., Herremans, T., Monseur, C. and Uyttendaele, S. (2007) *Étude exploratoire sur la mise en œuvre de nouvelles mesures visant à lutter contre les phénomènes de ségrégation scolaire et d'inéquité au sein du système éducatif de la Communauté française de Belgique,* Bruxelles: Rapport de recherche non publié.

Demeuse, M., Lafontaine, D. and Straeten, D. (2005) Parcours scolaire et inégalités de résultats, in M. Demeuse, A. Baye, M. Straeten, J. Nicaise, A. Matoul (eds), *Vers une école juste et efficace. 26 contributions sur les systèmes d'enseignement et de formation.* Bruxelles: De Boeck Université, collection 'Economie, Société, Région'.

DfES (2002) *Citizenship: The National Curriculum for England*, http://www.dfes.gov.uk/citizenship, accessed August 2003.

Dobozy, E. (2007) Effective learning of civic skills: Democratic schools succeed in nurturing the critical capabilities of pupils, *Educational Studies*, 33, 2, 115–128.

Dubet, F. (1999) Sentiments et jugements de justice dans l'expérience scolaire, in Meuret, D. (ed.), *La justice du système éducatif.* Paris: de Boeck.

Dubet, F. (2006) *Injustices*, Paris: Seuil.

Duffield, J., Allan, J., Turner, E. and Morris, B. (2000) Pupils' voices on achievement: An alternative to the standards agenda, *Cambridge Journal of Education*, 30, 2, 263–274.

Dupriez, V. and Dumray, X. (2006) Inequalities in school systems: Effect of school structure or of society structure? *Comparative Education*, 42, 2, 243–260.

Dupriez, V. and Vandenberghe, V. (2004) L'école en Communauté française de Belgique: de quelle inégalité parlons-nous? *Les Cahiers de la Recherche en Éducation et Formation*, 27, GIRSEF-UCL.

Dupriez, V. and Dumay, X. (2006) Élèves en difficulté d'apprentissage: parcours et environnements éducatifs différenciés en fonction des structures scolaires, *Les Cahiers de la Recherche en Éducation et Formation*, 51, GIRSEF-UCL.

Duru-Bellat, M. and Mingat, A. (1997) La constitution de classes de niveau dans les colleges, *Revue Francais de Sociologie*, 38, 759–789.

Education at a Glance (2007) http://www.oecd.org/document/30/0,3343,en_2649_39263238_39251550_1_1_1_1,00.html, accessed December 2008.

Ertl, H. (2006) European Union policies in education and training: The Lisbon agenda as a turning point, *Comparative Education*, 42, 1, 5–27.

European Group for Research on Equity in Educational Systems (2005) Equity in European Educational Systems: A set of indicators, *European Educational Research Journal*, 4, 2, 1–151.

European Group for Research on Equity in Educational Systems (2008) *Developing a Sense of Justice among Disadvantaged Students: The Role of Schools*, Birmingham: EGREES, 141.

Eurydice (2006) *National Summary Sheets on Education Systems in Europe and Ongoing Reforms*, Directorate-General for education and Culture, European Commission.

Eurydice (2007a) *The Information Network on Education in Europe*, http://www.eurydice.org/portal/page/portal/Eurydice, accessed January 2007.

Eurydice (2007b) *The Education System in the Czech Republic 2006/2007*, http://www.eurydice.org/ressources/eurydice/eurybase/pdf/0_integral/CZ_EN.pdf, accessed January 2007.

Euryidice (2008) http://eacea.ec.europa.eu/education/eurydice/index_en.php, accessed December 2008.

Ferguson, D. (2008) International trends in inclusive education: The continuing challenge to teach each one and everyone, *European Journal of Special Needs Education*, 23, 2, 109–120.

Fielding, M. and Bragg, S. (2003) *Pupils as Researchers: Making a Difference*, Cambridge: Pearson.

Fleurbaey, M. (1996) *Theories economiques de la justice*, Paris: Economica.

Gibbons, S. and Telhaj, S. (2006) *Peer Effects and Pupil Attainment: Evidence from Secondary School Transitions*, London: Centre for the Economics of Education, May.

Gibson, A. and Meuret, D. (1995) *The Development of Indicators on Equity in Education. OECD Measuring the Quality of Schools*, Paris: OECD, Center for Educational Research and Innovation.

Gilles, I. (2004) Croyance dans un monde juste et éducation, (330–333), in Toczek, MC et Martinot, D., *Le défi éducatif*, Paris: Armand Colin.

Glass, G. (2004) *Teacher Evaluation: Policy Brief*, Tempe, Az: Education Policy Research Unit.

Goldstein, H. (2008) Evidence and education policy – some reflections and allegations, *Cambridge Journal of Education*, 38, 3, 393–400.

Gorard, S. (1997) *School Choice in an Established Market*, Aldershot: Ashgate.

Gorard, S. (2000a) 'Underachievement' is still an ugly word: Reconsidering the relative effectiveness of schools in England and Wales, *Journal of Education Policy*, 15, 5, 559–573.

Gorard, S. (2000b) *Education and Social Justice*, Cardiff: University of Wales Press.

Gorard, S. (2001) International comparisons of school effectiveness: A second component of the 'crisis account'? *Comparative Education*, 37, 3, 279–296.

Gorard, S. (2005) Academies as the 'future of schooling': Is this an evidence-based policy? *Journal of Education Policy*, 20, 3, 369–377.

Gorard, S. (2006a) Value-added is of little value, *Journal of Educational Policy*, 21, 2, 233–241.

Gorard, S. (2006b) Is there a school mix effect? *Educational Review*, 58, 1, 87–94.

Gorard, S. (2006c) *Using Everyday Numbers Effectively in Research: Not a Book About Statistics*, London: Continuum.

Gorard, S. (2007a) Justice et equite a l'ecole: ce qu'en dissent les eleves dans les etudes internationales, *Revue Internationale d'Education Sevres*, 44, April, 79–84.

Gorard, S. (2007b) The true impact of school diversity, *International Journal for Education Law and Policy*, 2, 1–2, 35–40.

Gorard, S. (2008a) *Quantitative Research in education*, London: Sage.

Gorard, S. (2008b) Who is missing from higher education? *Cambridge Journal of Education*, 38, 3, 421–437.

Gorard, S. (2008c) The value-added of primary schools: What is it really measuring? *Educational Review*, 60, 2, 179–185.

Gorard, S. (2008d) Equity and its relationship to citizenship education, in J. Arthur, I. Davies and C. Hahn (eds), *The Sage Handbook of Education for Citizenship and Democracy*. London: Sage, 71–79.

Gorard, S. (2008e) Research impact is not always a good thing: A re-consideration of rates of 'social mobility' in Britain, *British Journal of Sociology of Education*, 29, 3, 317–324.

Gorard, S. (2009a) Misunderstanding and misrepresentation: A reply to Schagen and Hutchison, *International Journal of Research and Method in Education*, 32, 1, 3–12.

Gorard, S. (2009b) Measuring is more than assigning numbers, in G. Walford, E. Tucker and M. Viswanathan (eds), *Handbook of Measurement*. London: Sage.

Gorard, S. (2009c) Does the index of segregation matter? The composition of secondary schools in England since 1996, *British Educational Research Journal*, 35, 4, 639–652.

Gorard, S. (2009d) What are academies the answer to? *Journal of Education Policy*, 24, 1, 1–13.

Gorard, S. (2010a) Serious doubts about school effectiveness, *British Educational Research Journal*, http://www.informaworld.com/openurl?genre=article&issn=0141-1926&issue=preprint&spage=1&doi=10.1080/01411920903144251&date=2009&atitle=Serious doubts about school effectiveness&aulast=Gorard&aufirst=Stephen.

Gorard, S. (2010b) All evidence is equal: The flaw in statistical reasoning, *Oxford Review of Education*, March 2010.

Gorard, S., with Adnett, N., May, H., Slack, K., Smith, E. and Thomas, L. (2007) *Overcoming barriers to HE*, Stoke-on-Trent: Trentham.

Gorard, S., Lewis, J. and Smith, E. (2004) Disengagement in Wales: Educational, social and economic issues, *Welsh Journal of Education*, 13, 1, 118–147.

Gorard, S., Lumby, J., Briggs, A., Morrison, M., Hall, I., Maringe, F., See, B.H., Shaheen, R. and Wright, S. (2009a) *14–19 Reforms: QCA Centre Research Study, Commentary on the Baseline of Evidence 2007–2008*, London: QCA.

Gorard, S. and Rees, G. (2002) *Creating a Learning Society?* Bristol: Policy Press.

Gorard, S. and See, B.H. (2009) The impact of SES on participation and attainment in science, *Studies in Science Education*, 45, 1, 93–129.

Gorard, S., See, B.H. and Shaheen, R. (2009b) Educating for citizenship: Some lessons from England 2008, *Citizenship Teaching and Learning*, 5, 1, 35–45.

Gorard, S. and Selwyn, N. (2005) What makes a lifelong learner? *Teachers College Record*, 107, 6, 1193–1216.

Gorard, S. and Smith, E. (2004) An international comparison of equity in education systems? *Comparative Education*, 40, 1, 16–28.

Gorard, S. and Smith, E. (2007) Do barriers get in the way? A review of the determinants of post-16 participation, *Research in Post-Compulsory Education*, 12, 2, 141–158.

Gorard, S. and Smith, E. (2008) The impact of school experiences on pupils' sense of justice: An international study of pupil voice, *Orbis Scholae*, 2, 2, 87–105.

Gorard, S. and Taylor, C. (2002) What is segregation? A comparison of measures in terms of strong and weak compositional invariance, *Sociology*, 36, 4, 875–895.

Gorard, S., Taylor, C. and Fitz, J. (2003) *Schools, Markets and Choice Policies*, London: RoutledgeFalmer.

Gray, J. and Wilcox, B. (1995) *'Good School, Bad School': Evaluating Performance and Encouraging Improvement*, Buckingham: Open University Press.

Grayling, A. (2005) Two words of warning: Northern Ireland, *Times Educational Supplement*, 15 July, 9.

Grisay, A. (1997) *Evolution des acquis cognitifs et socio-affectifs des élèves au cours des années de collège*, MEN-Direction de l'Evaluation et de la Prospective, Dossiers Education et formations, 88.

Guldemond, H. and Bosker, R. (2009) School effects on pupils' progress – a dynamic perspective, *School Effectiveness and School Improvement*, 20, 2, 255–268.

Haahr, J., with Nielsen, T., Hansen, E. and Jakobsen, S. (2005) *Explaining Pupil Performance: Evidence from the International PISA, TIMSS and PIRLS Surveys*, Danish Technological Institute, www.danishtechnology.dk, accessed August 2005.

Halstead, J. and Taylor, M. (2000) Learning and Teaching about Values: A Review of Recent Research, *Cambridge Journal of Education*, 30, 2, 169–202.

Hamill, P. and Boyd, B. (2002) Equality, fairness and rights – the young person's voice, *British Journal of Special Education* 29, 3, 111–117.

Hand, M. (2006) Against autonomy as an educational aim, *Oxford Review of Education*, 32, 4, 535–550.

Harris, N. and Gorard, S. (2009) The United Kingdom, in *The Education Systems of Europe*, London: Sage.

Heitmeyer, W. and Legge, S. (2008) Youth, violence, and social disintegration, in *New Directions for Youth Development*, 119, Fall, San Francisco: Jossey-Bass.

Hirsch, D. (2002) Divide and you will divide again, *The Times Educational Supplement*, 13 December, 19.

Horn, D. (2009) Age of selection counts: A cross-country analysis of educational institutions, *Educational Research and Evaluation*, 15, 4, 343–366.

Howard, S. and Gill, J. (2000) The pebble in the pond: Children's constructions of power, politics and democratic citizenship, *Cambridge Journal of Education*, 30, 3, 357–378.

Hoyle, R. and Robinson, J. (2003) League tables and school effectiveness: A mathematical model, *Proceedings of the Royal Society of London B*, 270, 113–199.

Huang, M. (2009) Beyond horse race comparisons of national performance averages, *Educational Research and Evaluation*, 15, 4, 327–342.

Hutmacher, W., Cochrane, D., Bottani, N. (2001) (eds) *In Pursuit of Equity in Education. Using International Indicators to Compare Equity Policies*, Dordrecht: Kluwer Academic.

Jansen, T., Chioncel, N. and Dekkers, H. (2006) Social cohesion and integration: Learning active citizenship, *British Journal of Sociology of Education*, 27, 2, 189–205.

Kellerhals, J., Coenen-Huther, J. and Modak, M. (1988) *Figures de l'équité*, Paris: Presses universitaires de France.

Kelly, S. (2009) Social identity theories and educational engagement, *British Journal of Sociology of Education*, 30, 4, 449–462.

Kelly, S. and Monczunski, L. (2007) Overcoming the volatility in school-level gain scores: A new approach to identifying value-added with cross-sectional data, *Educational Researcher*, 36, 5, 279–287.

Kendall, L., Golden, S., Machin, S., McNally, S., Meghir, C., Morris, M., Noden, P., O'Donnell, L., Ridley, K., Rutt, S., Schagen, I., Stoney, S. and West, A. (2005) *Excellence in Cities: The National Evaluation of a Policy to Raise Standards in Urban Schools 2000–2003*, DfES Research Report 675A.

Kerr, D. (2003) Citizenship education in England: The making of a new subject. *Online Journal for Social Science Education*, http://www.sowi-onlinejournal. de/2003–2/england_kerr.htm

Kyriakides, L. (2008) Testing the validity of the comprehensive model of educational effectiveness: A step towards the development of a dynamic model of effectiveness, *School Effectiveness and School Improvement*, 19, 4, 429–446.

Leckie, G. and Goldstein, H. (2009) *The Limitations of Using School League Tables to Inform School Choice*, Working Paper 09/208, Bristol: Centre for Market and Public Organisation.

Lee, M. and Madyun, N. (2008) School racial composition and academic achievement: The case of Hmong LEP pupils in the USA, *Educational Studies*, 34, 4, 319–331.

Lerner, J. (1980) *The Belief in a Just World: A Fundamental Delusion*, New York: Plenum Press.

Levin, H. (2009) The economic payoff to investing in educational justice, *Educational Researcher*, 38, 1, 5–20.

Lewis, A. (2004) 'And when did you last see your father?' exploring the views of children with learning difficulties/disabilities, *British Journal of Special Education*, 31, 1, 3–9.

Lewis, A., Parsons, S. and Robertson, C. (2006) *My school, My Family, My Life: Telling it Like it Is*, Stratford-upon-Avon: Disability Rights Commission.

Lizzio, A., Wilson, K. and Hadaway, V. (2007) University pupils' perceptions of a fair learning environment: A social justice perspective, *Assessment and Evaluation in Higher Education*, 32, 2, 195–213.

Lubienski, S. and Lubienski, C. (2006) School sector and academic achievement@ a multi-level analysis of NAEP Mathematics data, *American Educational Research Journal*, 43, 4, 651–698.

Lumby, J., Gorard, S., Morrison, M. and Rose, A. (2004) *Review of Level Three Provision in North Torfaen*, Cwmbran: Torfaen LEA.

Lumby, J., Gorard, S., Morrison, M., Smith, E., Lewis, G. and Middlewood, D. (2006) *14–19 Arrangements in Cardiff: Review and Recommendations*, Cardiff: LEA.

Luyten, H., Schildkamp, K. and Folmer, E. (2009) Cognitive development in Dutch primary education, the impact of individual background and classroom composition, *Educational Research and Evaluation*, 15, 3, 265–283.

Lynn, R. (1988) *Educational Achievement in Japan: Lessons for the West*, London: Macmillan Press.

Macleod, F. and Lambe, P. (2008) Dynamics of adult participation in part-time education and training: Results from the British Household Panel Survey, *Research Papers in Education*, 23, 2, 231–241.

Mansell, W. (2005) Don't mention the troubles, *Times Educational Supplement*, 18 February, 16.

Mansell, W. (2006) Shock of low score drives heads to resign, *Times Educational Supplement*, 9 June, 6.

Manzo, K. (2002) Japanese school children 'cram' to boost achievement, *Education Week*, 7 August, 14.

Marks, G., Cresswell, J. and Ainley, J. (2006) Explaining socioeconomic inequalities in pupil achievement, *Educational Research and Evaluation*, 12, 2, 105–128.

Marley, D. (2009) A third of schools bore their classes, *Times Educational Supplement*, 9 January, 12.

Marsh, H., Trautwein, U., Ludtke, O., Baumert, J. and Koller, O. (2007) The big-fish-little-pond effects of selective high schools on self-concept after graduation, *American Educational Research Journal*, 44, 3, 631–669.

Massey, D. and Fischer, M. (2006) The effect of childhood segregation on minority academic performance at selective colleges, *Ethnic and Racial Studies*, 29, 1, 1–26.

Matějů, P. and Straková, J. (2005) The role of the family and the school in the reproduction of educational inequalities in the post-Communist Czech Republic, *British Journal of Sociology of Education*, 26, 1, 15–38.

McBeath, J., Demetriou, H., Rudduck, J. and Myers, K. (2003) *Consulting Pupils: A Toolkit for Teachers*. Cambridge: Pearson.

McGaw, B. (2008) The role of the OECD in international comparative studies of achievement, *Assessment in Education*, 15, 3, 223–243.

McIntyre, D., Pedder, D. and Rudduck, J. (2005) Pupil voice: Comfortable and uncomfortable learnings for teachers, *Research Papers in Education*, 20, 2, 149–168.

Merle, P. (2005) *L'élève humilié*, Paris: PUF.

Meuret, D. (2001) School equity as a matter of justice, in W. Hutmacher, D. Cochrane, N. Bottani (eds), *In Pursuit of Equity in Education*. Dordrecht: Kluwer Academic.

Meuret, D. and Desvignes, S. (2005) *Le sentiment de justice des élèves d'après PISA 2000 et 2003*, Dijon: Université de Bourgogne.

Meuret, D. and Marivain, T. (1997) Inégalités de bien être au collège, *Les Dossiers d'Education et Formation*, 89.

Nash, R. (2003) Is the school composition effect real? A discussion with evidence from the UK PISA data, *School Effectiveness and School Improvement*, 14, 4, 441–457.

Newton, P. (1997) Measuring comparability of standards across subjects: Why our statistical techniques do not make the grade, *British Educational Research Journal*, 23, 4, 433–449.

Newton, P. (2009) The reliability of results from national curriculum testing in England, *Educational Research*, 51, 2, 181–212.

Nicaise, I. (2000) *The Right to Learn: Educational Strategies for Socially Excluded Youth in Europe*, Bristol: Policy Press.

Nicaise, J., Straeten, M., Baye, A. and Demeuse, M. (2005) Comment développer un système d'indicateurs d'équité au niveau européen? in M. Demeuse, A. Baye, M. Straeten, J. Nicaise and A. Matoul (eds), *Vers une école juste et efficace. 26 contributions sur les systèmes d'enseignement et de formation*, Coll. Economie, Société, Région, De Boeck, Bruxelles, 337–353.

Normand, R. (2008) School effectiveness or the horizon of the world as a laboratory, *British Journal of Sociology of Education*, 29, 6, 665–676.

Norwich, B. and Kelly, N. (2004) Pupils' views on inclusion: Moderate learning difficulties and bullying in mainstream and special schools, *British Educational Research Journal*, 30, 1, 43–65.

Noyes, A. (2005) Pupil voice: Purpose, power and the possibilities for democratic schooling, *British Educational Research Journal*, 31, 4, 533–540.

Nucci, L. (2001) *Education in the Moral Domain*, Cambridge: Cambridge University Press.

Nuttall, D. (1979) The myth of comparability, *Journal of the National Association of Inspectors and Advisers*, 11, 16–18.

Nuttall, D., Goldstein, H., Presser, R. and Rasbash, H. (1989) Differential school effectiveness, *International Journal of Educational Research*, 13, 7, 769–776.

OECD (2005) *Regards sur l'éducation. Les indicateurs de l'OECD 2005*, OECD, Paris.

OECD (2007a) *Education at a Glance. OECD Indicators 2007*. OECD, Paris.

OECD (2007b) *The Programme for International Pupil Assessment* (PISA), http://www.pisa.oecd.org/pages/0,2987,en_32252351_32235731_1_1_1_1_1,00.html, Accessed January 2007.

OFSTED (2007) *Ofsted TellUs2 Survey Summary and Technical Manual*, http://www.ttrb.ac.uk/viewArticle2.aspx?contentId=14193, accessed 7 January 2009.

Opp, G. (2007) Inclusion of pupils with disabilities in German schools, *Educational and Child Psychology*, 24, 3, 8.

Osler, A. (2000) Children's rights, responsibilities and understandings of school discipline, *Research Papers in Education*, 15, 1, 49–67.

Osler, A. and Starkey, H. (2006) Education for democratic citizenship: A review of research, policy and practice 1995–2005, *Research Papers in Education*, 21, 4, 433–466.

Park (2000) *Voodoo science*, Oxford: Oxford University Press.

Paterson, L. (2009) Civic values and the subject matter of educational courses, *Oxford Review of Education*, 35, 1, 81–98.

Polesel, J. (2008) Democratising the curriculum or training the children of the poor: School-based vocational training in Australia, *Journal of Education Policy*, 23, 6, 615–632.

Pomeroy, E. (1999) The teacher-pupil relationship in secondary school: Insights from excluded pupils, *British Journal of Sociology of Education* 20, 4, 465–482.

Print, M. and Coleman, D. (2003) Towards understanding of social capital and citizenship education, *Cambridge Journal of Education*, 33, 1, 123–149.

Pugh, K. and Bergin, D. (2005) The effect of schooling on pupils' out-of-school experience, *Educational Researcher*, 34, 9, 15–23.

QCA (1998) *Education for Citizenship and the Teaching of Democracy in Schools, Final report of the advisory group on citizenship*, London: QCA.

Raty, H., Kasanen, K. and Laine, N. (2009) Parents' participation in their child's schooling, *Educational Research*, 53, 3, 277–293.

Rawls, J. (1971) *A Theory of Justice*, Oxford: Oxford University Press.

Reay, D. (2006) 'I'm not seen as one of the clever children': Consulting primary school pupils about the social conditions of learning. *Educational Review*, 58, 2, 171–181.

Repères et Références Statistiques, MEN, 2007, http://www.education.gouv.fr/cid21641/reperes-et-references-statistiques.htm, accessed July 2009.

Riley, K. (2004) Voices of disaffected pupils: Implications for policy and practice. *British Journal of Educational Studies*, 52, 2, 166–179.

Roemer, J. (1996) *Theories of Distributive Justice*, Cambridge, MA: Harvard University Press.

Roesgaard, M. (1998) *Moving Mountains: Japanese Education Reform*, Denmark: Aarhus University Press.

Rose, R., Fletcher, W. and Goodwin, G. (1999) Pupils with severe learning difficulties as personal target setters, *British Journal of Special Education*, 26, 4, 206–212.

Rose, R. and Shevlin, M. (2004) Encouraging voices: Listening to young people who have been marginalised, *Support for Learning*, 19, 4, 155–161.

Rumberger, R. and Palardy, G. (2005) Test scores, dropout rate, and transfer rates as alternative indicators of high school performance, *American Educational Research Journal*, 42, 1, 3–42.

Rutter, M., Maughan, B., Mortimore, P. and Ouston, J. (1979). *Fifteen Thousand Hours: Secondary Schools and their Effects on Children*, London: Open Books.

Sanders, W. (2000) Value-added assessment from pupil achievement data, *Journal of Personnel Evaluation in Education*, 14, 4, 329–339.

Sanders, W. and Horn, S. (1998) Research findings from the Tennessee value-added assessment system (TVAAS) database, *Journal of Personnel Evaluation in Education*, 12, 3, 247–256.

Sanders, W. and Rivers, J. (1996) *Cumulative and Residual Effects of Teachers on Future Pupil Academic Achievement*, University of Tennessee: Value-Added Research and Assessment Center.

Schagen, I. (2002) Attitudes to citizenship in England: Multilevel statistical analysis of the IEA civics data, *Research Papers in Education*, 17, 3, 229–259.

Schutz, G., Ursprung, H. and Wobmann, L. (2008) Education policy and equality of opportunity, *Kyklos*, 61, 2.

Selwyn, N., Gorard, S. and Furlong, J. (2006) *Adult Learning in the Digital Age*, London: RoutledgeFalmer.

Shamir, A. (2007) Inclusion from theory to practice: General and local issues, *Educational and Child Psychology*, 24, 3, 37.

Shipman, M. (1997) *The Limitations of Social Research*, Harlow: Longman.

Sirota, R. (1988) *L'ecole primaire au quotidien*, Paris: Presses Universitaires de France.

Slee, R. (2001) Driven to the margins: Disabled pupils, inclusive schooling and the politics of possibility, *Cambridge Journal of Education*, 31, 3, 385–397.

Smith, A. (2003) Citizenship education in Northern Ireland: Beyond national identity, *Cambridge Journal of Education*, 33, 1, 15–31.

Smith, E. (2009) What can secondary data tell us about school exclusions? *International Journal of Research and Method in Education*, 32, 1, 89–101.

Smith, E. and Gorard, S. (2006) Pupils' views of equity in education, *Compare*, 36, 1, 41–56.

Smith, P. and Street, A. (2006) *Analysis of Secondary School Efficiency: Final Report*, DfES Research Report 788.

Somekh, S. (2001) Methodological issues in identifying and describing the way knowledge is constructed with and without information and communications technology, *Journal of Information Technology for Teacher Education*, 10 (1 and 2), 157–178.

Spender, D. (1982) *Invisible Women: The Schooling Scandal*, London: Women's Press.

Sreekanth, Y. (2009) Bullying: An element accentuating social segregation, *Education 3–13*, 37, 3, 233–245.

Stevens, P. (2009) Pupils' perspectives on racism and differential treatment by teachers, *British Educational Research Journal*, 35, 3, 413–430.

Stewart, W. (2008) Pupil voice to become law, *Times Educational Supplement*, 14 November, 1.

Stewart, W. (2009) 'Appalling' failures of English test markers, *The Times Educational Supplement*, 30 March, 14.

Straková, J. (2003) International large-scale studies of educational achievement – the involvement of the Czech Republic, *Czech Sociological Review*, 39, 3, 411–424.

Strand, S. and Winston, J. (2008) Educational aspirations in inner city schools, *Educational Studies*, 34, 4, 249–267.

Tangen, R. (2008) Listening to children's voices in educational research: Some theoretical and methodological problems, *European Journal of Special Needs Education*, 23, 2, 157–166.

Tannock, S. (2008) The problem of education-based discrimination, *British Journal of Sociology of Education*, 29, 5, 439–449.

TES (2006) Why some schools still need 'a bit of a kicking', *Times Educational Supplement*, 23 June, 18.

Themelis, S. (2008) Meritocracy through education and social mobility in post-war Britain: A critical examination, *British Journal of Sociology of Education*, 29, 5, 427–438.

Thomas, G. and Loxley, A. (2007) *Deconstructing Special Education and Constructing Inclusion*, Maidenhead: Open University Press.

Thomas, S., Peng, W.J. and Gray, J. (2007) Modelling patterns of improvement over time: Value-added trends in English secondary school performance across ten cohorts, *Oxford Review of Education*, 33, 3, 261–295.

Thomas, W. and Webber, D. (2009) Choice at 16: School, parental and peer group effects, *Research in Post-Compulsory Education*, 14, 2, 119–141.

Thornberg, R. (2008) School children's reasoning about school rules, *Research Papers in Education*, 23, 1, 37–52.

Torney-Purta, J., Lehmann, R., Oswald, H. and Schulz, W. (2001) Citizenship and education in twenty-eight countries: Civic knowledge and engagement at age 14, Amsterdam: IEA.

Trannoy, A. (1999) Social dominance egalitarianism and utilitariaris, *Revue Economique*, 50, 4, 733–755.

Tymms, P. (2003) *School Composition Effects*, School of Education, Durham University, January.
Tymms, P. and Dean, C. (2004) *Value-Added in the Primary School League Tables: A Report for the National Association of Head Teachers*, Durham: CEM Centre.
Tymms, P., Merrell, C., Heron, T., Jones, P., Alborne, S. and Henderson, B. (2008) The importance of districts, *School Effectiveness and School Improvement*, 19, 3, 261–274.
Van de Grift, W. (2009) Reliability and validity in measuring the value added of schools, *School Effectiveness and School Improvement*, 20, 2, 269–285.
Vandenberghe, V. (2000) Enseignement et iniquité: singularité de la question en Communauté Wallonie-Bruxelles, *Les Cahiers de Recherche du GIRSEF*, 8.
Walford, G. (2004) No discrimination on the basis of irrelevant qualifications, *Cambridge Journal of Education*, 34, 3, 353–361.
Walker, J. (2009) The inclusion and construction of the worthy citizen through lifelong learning: A focus on the OECD, *Journal of Education Policy*, 24, 3, 335–351.
Webber, R. and Butler, T. (2007) Classifying pupils by where they live: How well does this predict variations in their GCSE results? *Urban Studies*, 44, 7, 1229–1253.
West, A. and Hind, A. (2006) Selectivity, admissions and intakes to 'comprehensive' schools in London, England, *Educational Studies*, 32, 2, 145–155.
Whitehead, J. and Clough, N. (2004) Pupils: The forgotten partners in education action zones, *Journal of Education Policy* 19, 2, 215–227.
Whitehead, M. (1991) The concepts and principles of equity and health, *Health Promotion International*, 6, 3, 217–228.
Wilson, A. (1959) Residential segregation of social classes and aspirations of high school boys, *American Sociological Review*, 24, 836–845.
Wood, E. (2003) The power of pupil perspectives in evidence-based practice: The case of gender and underachievement, *Research Papers in Education*, 18, 4, 365–383.
Wyness, M. (2006) Children, young people and civic participation: Regulation and local diversity, *Educational Review* 58, 2, 209–218.
Younger, M. and Warrington, M. (2009) Mentoring and target-setting in a secondary school in England, *Oxford Review of Education*, 35, 2, 169–185.

Index